Joseph A. Fleck

1892–1977

Joseph Fleck saw art as a means of giving pleasure to the eye. Initially he painted New Mexico's landscapes and the Spanish people and Indians in a straightforward, rather crisp academic style, a style that had given him recognition as a portraitist. As he became more attuned to the strong light of Taos and the marvelous clouds that pass rapidly overhead in the region, he flared out his brushes to create more impressionistic images. His brightly colored, luminous landscapes reflect the warmth of summer, as well as the gold of the leaves touched by frost in the fall.

Van Deren Coke

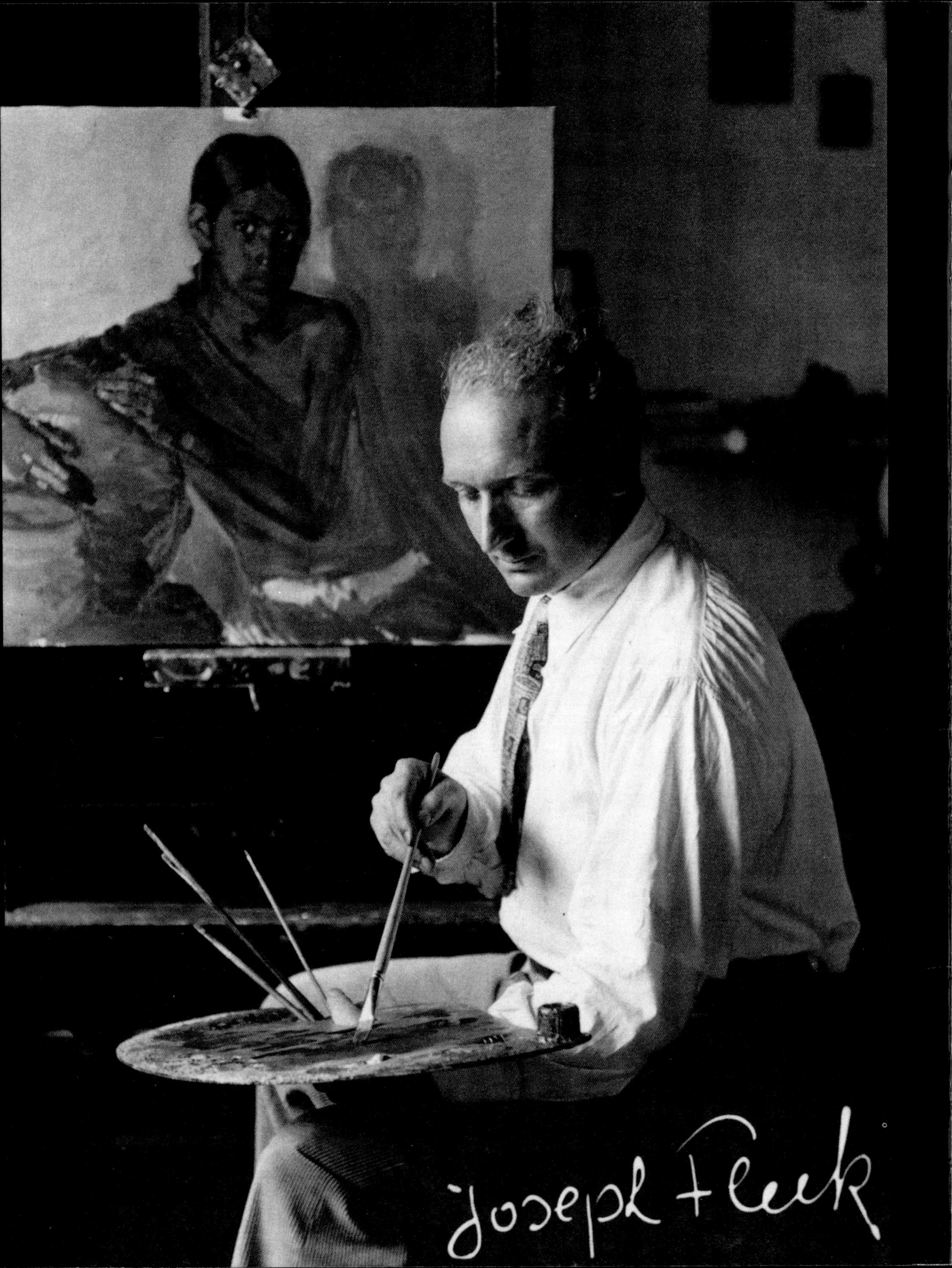

Joseph Fleck

JOSEPH A. FLECK
AN EARLY TAOS PAINTER

Museum of Fine Arts, Museum of New Mexico

This publication was made possible through the generosity of Joseph A. Fleck, Jr.

Cover: *Fiesta Array,* 1929, oil, 50" x 46"; The Carl and Elisabeth Waldo Dentzel Collection; photographed by Ken Veeder, North Hollywood.
Frontispiece: Joseph A. Fleck, 1931; photograph by C. E. Lord.
Photographs in the biographical sketch chapter are from the Collection of Joseph A. Fleck, Jr.

Printed in the United States of America.

Library of Congress Cataloging in Publication Data

Fleck, Joseph A.
Joseph A. Fleck, an early Taos painter.

Other museums participating in the exhibition:
Roswell Museum and Art Center, Roswell, N.M.; Oklahoma Art Center, Oklahoma City; Museum of Art of the American West, Houston, Tex.; Museum of the Southwest, Midland, Tex.; Panhandle-Plains Historical Museum, Canyon, Tex.; McAllen International Museum, McAllen, Tex.
Contents: Preface / by David G. Turner—Joseph A. Fleck, a biographical sketch / by Sandra D'Emilio—The paintings of Joseph A. Fleck / by Joseph Armstrong Baird, Jr.—[etc.]
1. Fleck, Joseph A., 1892–1977—Exhibitions. 2. Taos school of art—Exhibitions. I. D'Emilio, Sandra, 1939– II. Baird, Joseph Armstrong, 1922– . III. Museum of New Mexico. Museum of Fine Arts. IV. Title.
ND237.F475A4 1985 759.13 85-2980
ISBN 0-89013-152-X

Contents

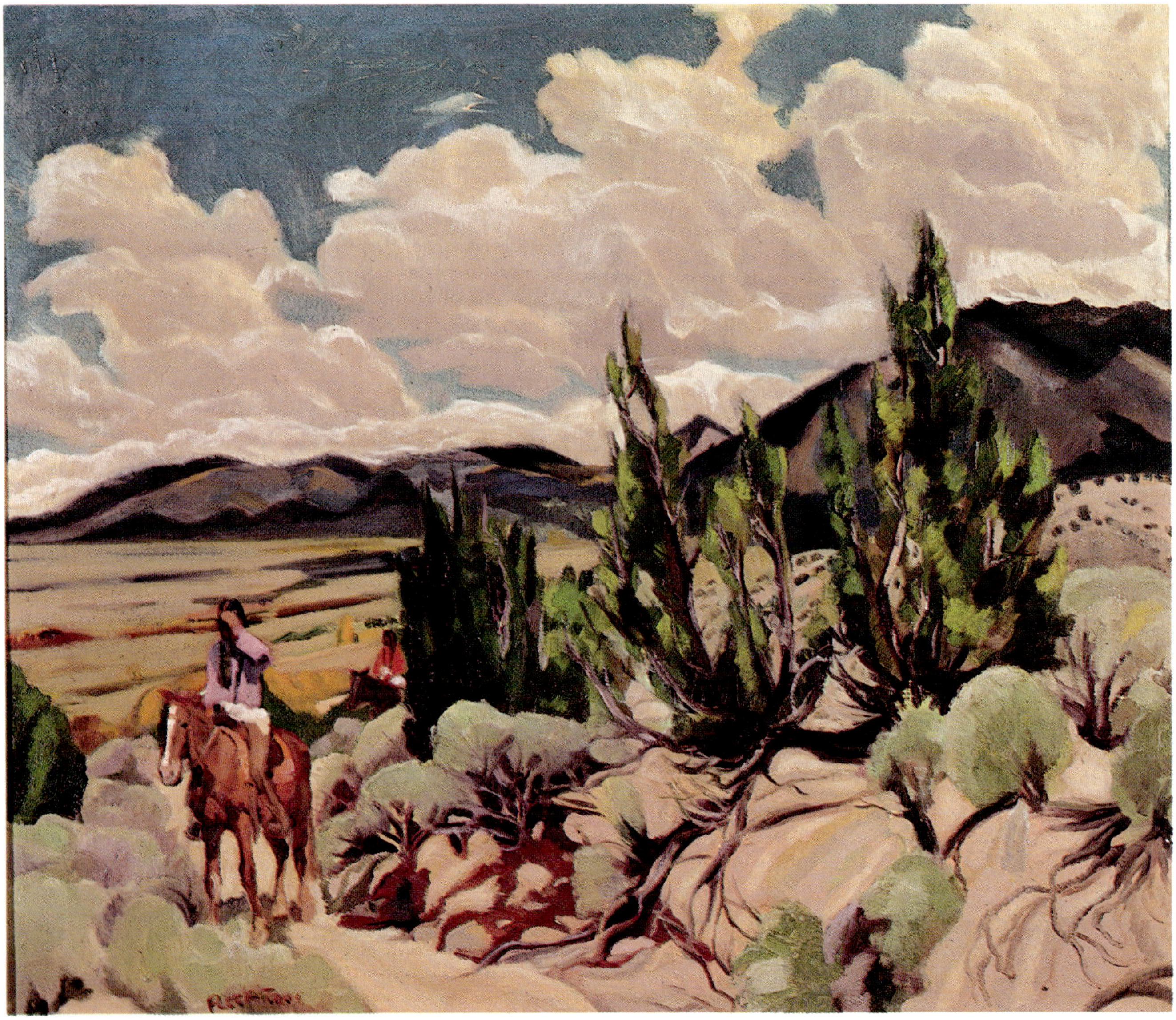

PEACEFUL HUNT 1936
Oil 25" x 30"
The Harmsen Collection

Preface

Museums are fortunate to be in the position of contributing insights to the study of art history. The very nature of a museum encourages the pursuit of discovery—finding new material about or by an artist and exhibiting it in a context that provides for a greater understanding of the artist and the period in which he or she worked. As this material is published in an exhibition catalog, a permanent record is made of the work, which when added to library and museum collections, can become a valued addition to the literature of art history.

This exhibition and catalog, *Joseph A. Fleck: An Early Taos Painter,* is the product of one of those opportunities to rediscover an artist after his death and examine a large body of his work, specifically in the context of the Taos, New Mexico, painters with whom he aligned himself. Joseph Fleck's career covered a wide geographic region—from Vienna, Austria, to Kansas City, Missouri, to Taos, New Mexico—and took place at a time when American painters were gaining their confidence and independence as contemporary artists. The work in this exhibition focuses on Fleck's interaction with the New Mexico landscape and also features many fine portraits, which he called "flowers of the desert." These paintings of Taos-area natives, with their copper skin and dark hair, are beautiful and exotic.

In assembling this exhibition, many people have worked together for its success. I greatly appreciate the efforts of Sandra D'Emilio, Curator of Paintings at the Museum of Fine Arts, who has organized the show and written a biographical essay for the catalog, and of Dr. Joseph A. Baird, Jr., Professor of Art History at the University of California, Davis, in writing an informative analysis of Joseph A. Fleck's paintings. This project could not have been realized without the guidance and financial support of Joseph A. Fleck, Jr., who was extremely generous with his resources and knowledge about his father's career. I also thank Mr. Lewis L. Dail for his financial contribution. For their work in installing the exhibition and publishing the catalog, I also wish to thank John Tinker, Fine Arts Preparator; Sue Critchfield and Claudia Gayheart for their help with loan arrangements; Marmika, Exhibitions Graphics; and Jim Mafchir and Sarah Nestor, Museum Publications.

An exhibition of this scope also requires the generosity of collectors. For agreeing to part with their pieces for more than a year, the Museum thanks the following institutions and private collectors: The Nelson-Atkins Museum of Art, Kansas City, Missouri; Oklahoma Art Center, Oklahoma City; El Paso Museum of Art, Texas; University Art Museum, University of New Mexico, Albuquerque; The Harwood Foundation Museum of Taos Art, New Mexico; The Collection of Western Art and Artifacts of Business Men's Assurance Company of America, Kansas City, Missouri; New Mexico State Fair, Albuquerque; The Carl and Elisabeth Waldo Dentzel Collection, Northridge, California; The Harmsen Collection, Denver, Colorado; Joseph A. Fleck, Jr., Livermore, California; Michael J. Ross, St. Louis, Missouri; Mr. and Mrs. Joseph Szymanski, Pasadena, California; Lewis L. Dail, Kansas City, Missouri; and Mr. and Mrs. Robert E. McKee III, Dallas, Texas.

After the exhibition's showing in Santa Fe, the paintings will travel to six other museums in the Southwest, and we wish to thank the following people for their participation in this tour: Wendell Ott, Director, Roswell Museum and Art Center, Roswell, New Mexico; William G. Riggs, Assistant Curator, Oklahoma Art Center, Oklahoma City; Samuel H. Grove, Director, Museum of Art of the American West, Houston, Texas; Sue Devine, Curator, Museum of the Southwest, Midland, Texas; Bruce Hartman, Curator of Art, Panhandle-Plains Historical Museum, Canyon, Texas; Jerry W. Moore, Exhibition Coordinator, McAllen International Museum, McAllen, Texas.

David G. Turner
Associate Director
Museum of Fine Arts, Museum of New Mexico

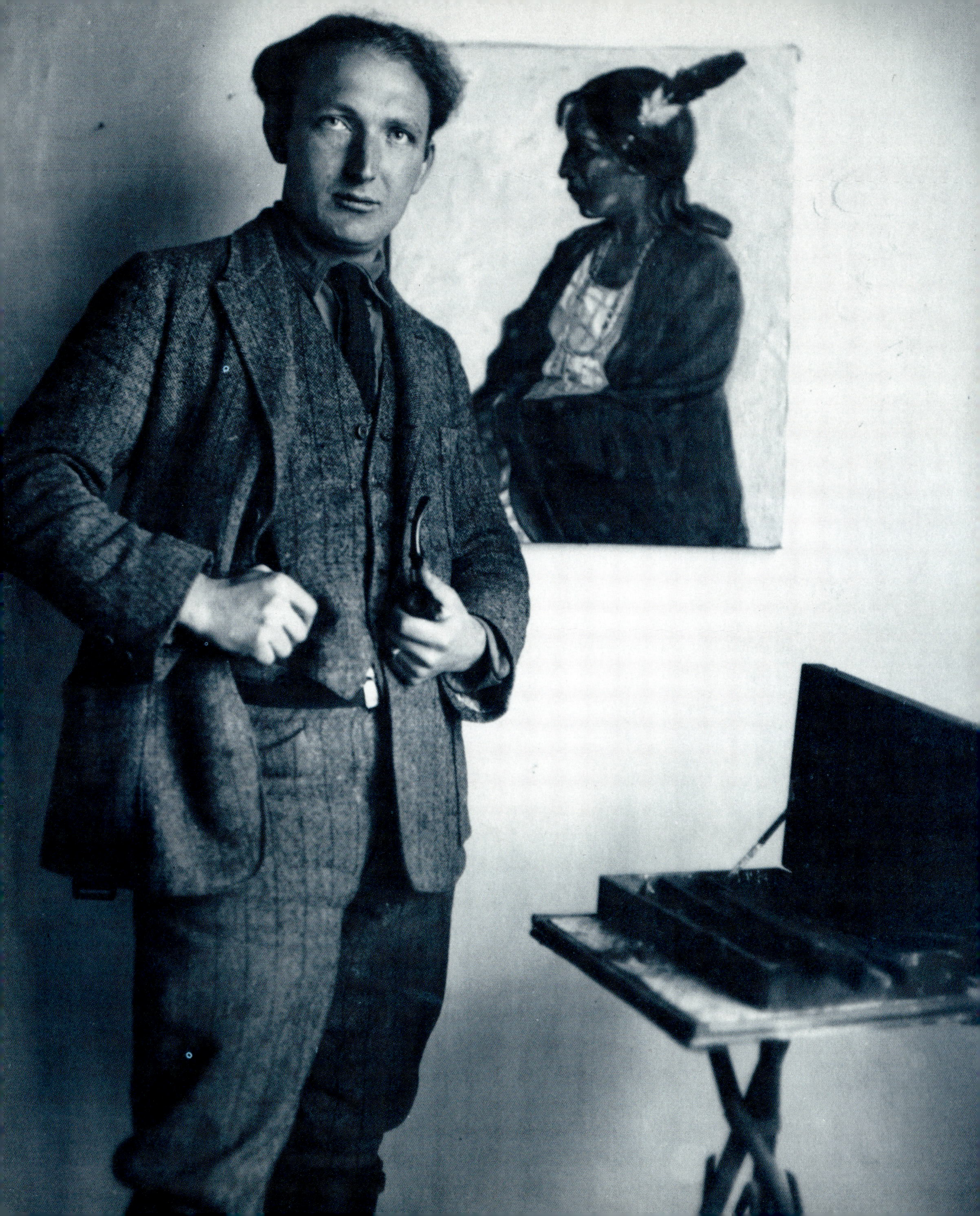

Joseph A. Fleck

A Biographical Sketch

Joseph Amadeus Fleck arrived in Kansas City from Vienna in May 1922 knowing only a few words of English. His baggage consisted of one suitcase and a roll of etchings tucked under one arm. Because of the disastrous economic conditions prevailing in postwar Austria, Fleck had been forced to borrow money for his steerage passage to America from a Kansas City friend. With the help of Conrad Hug, an art dealer and gallery owner, Fleck obtained a job with the Tiffany stained-glass factory in Kansas City and within a year became its head designer. After he learned to speak English, his charming outgoing manner enabled him to make some important social contacts, which helped him begin a successful portrait-painting career.

Born August 25, 1892, in the small village of Siegless in the province of Burgenland, Austria, Fleck as a schoolchild amazed his teachers with his drawing skills. In his teens, he apprenticed to an ornamental engraver. Fleck completed his studies with a bas-relief of Emperor Franz Joseph that so impressed the instructor that he recommended Fleck for a scholarship to the Vienna Royal Academy of Fine Arts in 1912.

The onset of World War I interrupted Fleck's academy studies. He was drafted into the Austro-Hungarian army and shipped to the Carpathian front. Word of his artistic abilities spread throughout the regiment, and soon he was spending most of his time painting the officers. Fleck often said he owed his survival during the war to his artistic talent. Later he returned to Vienna to become an official government artist. In this capacity, he painted war scenes and portraits of important government and military officials. Near the end of the war, however, Fleck was able to enter what was then called the Vienna Academy of Fine Arts, where he completed his studies with distinction in 1920.

In 1924, Fleck discovered Taos in Kansas City's Hug Gallery, where an exhibition of paintings by the Taos Society of Artists was being held. The Taos landscape and the exotic Indians and Hispanic people fascinated him. As a child in Vienna, he had delighted in reading about the American West. The same year he saw the exhibition, he decided to visit Taos and view it for himself.

Fleck arrived in Taos in the summer and soon felt at home among its diverse inhabitants—Hispanics, Indians, and a few Anglos. He began lasting friendships with many of the artists whose paintings he had admired in Kansas City. Among these were E. Martin Hennings, Ernest L. Blumenschein, Bert G. Phillips, E. Irving Couse, W. Herbert Dunton, Oscar E. Berninghaus, and Walter Ufer. Fleck also began a lifelong friendship with Leon Gaspard. During this first trip to Taos, Fleck worked at a furious pace, filling numerous canvases with the Taos landscape, the Indian and Hispanic people, and their architectures. Included in this exhibition are three paintings from this first trip to Taos; these are *Sunny Corner* (p. 14), painted from the porch of Irving Couse's studio, *Spanish Cowboy* (p. 23), and *House in the Sun* (p. 24).

Fleck spent a great deal of time with E. Martin Hennings, who was also a bachelor. They painted together and often took trips to the mountains to paint the aspens. Hennings and Fleck's friendship and painting trips continued after their marriages. Often they would camp with their families at Twining, now known as Taos Ski Basin.

In late 1924, Fleck returned to Kansas City, where he held an exhibition of his Taos paintings at his studio on Knickerbocker Place. Six months later, in 1925, he packed up his paints and brushes and returned to Taos. This move was permanent.

The move was not the only change that took

Fleck in Taos studio, 1924.

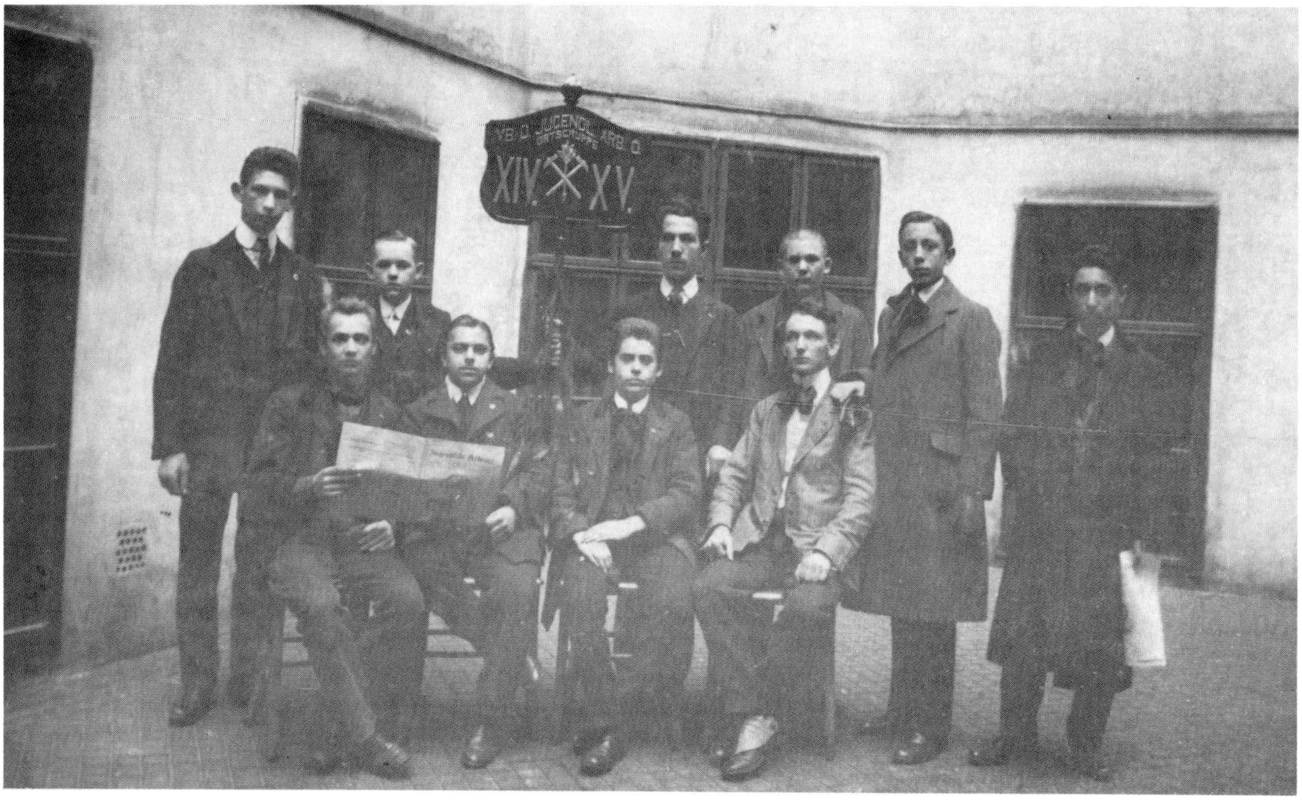

Fleck (front right) with classmates at the Royal Academy of Fine Arts in Vienna, 1914.

place in Fleck's life. While in Kansas City early in 1925, he had met Mable Davidson Mantz, who came from a wealthy Texas family. She had graduated from the New England Conservatory and had spent many years living abroad. Her father, a wealthy financier, did business in Texas and Kansas City. Mable arrived at the railroad station in Lamy, New Mexico, and on July 16, 1925, the Flecks were married in Santa Fe by a justice of the peace. Fleck, when describing the event in his charming Viennese accent, referred to the latter as the "justice of the pieces." Through Mable, he met many prominent people whose portraits he would eventually paint.

The newly married couple made their home in Taos, where they later built a large pueblo-style adobe home alongside the original Santa Fe trail on La Loma, about a half mile from the Taos Plaza. Through the large picture window in his studio, Fleck had a perfect view of Taos Pueblo Mountain, which must have been a constant source of inspiration to him.

In 1926, the Flecks toured Europe on their honeymoon, visiting Paris, Vienna, Italy, and Yugoslavia. In 1930, two years after the birth of their son, Joseph A. Fleck, Jr., the Flecks began a second tour of Europe, visiting Paris, Vienna, Italy, and Spain. Fleck painted for two months in Toledo, Spain, where he produced several monumental canvases containing views of the city. The trip culminated with a successful exhibition at the Galerie Bernheim-Jeune in Paris, which featured paintings from Taos and the recent visit to Spain.

The years between 1923 and 1931 were both productive and successful for Fleck. He was awarded the Bronze Medal of the Kansas City Art Institute in 1923, the Morris Rosenwald Prize of the Chicago Art Institute in 1927, and the Silver Medal of the Kansas City Art Institute in 1929. He held a one-man exhibition at the Houston Museum of Fine Arts in 1930 and was represented in group exhibitions at the

Pennsylvania Academy of Fine Arts and the Cincinnati Art Museum in 1926. He was also represented at the Carnegie International Exhibition in Pittsburgh in 1928.

Upon his return from Europe in 1931, Fleck found that economic conditions had changed drastically for the worse. The Depression was already under way, and the next ten years would be difficult for him both financially and spiritually. Frequent trips became necessary to Kansas City and Texas in search of portrait commissions. The WPA program offered help with commissions for murals in the post offices of Raton, New Mexico, and Hugo, Oklahoma. Despite the desperate economic conditions, Fleck's creativity did not ebb. Among his noteworthy paintings of this period are *The Guitarist* (p. 32), exhibited at the New York World's Fair in 1939, and *Two Spanish Musicians* (p. 33).

Life was changing in Taos. The Taos Society of Artists had disbanded in 1927, and the Don Fernando Hotel, the artists' favorite meeting place,

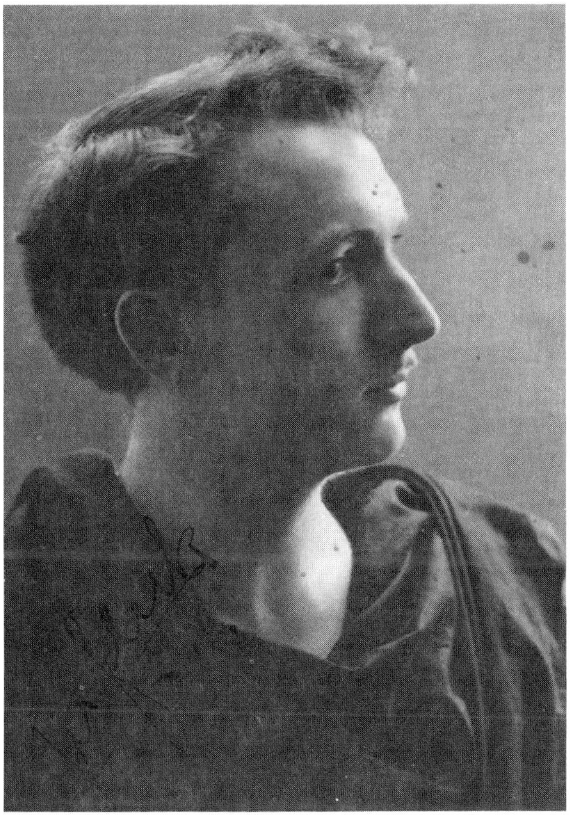

Profile of Fleck, 1916.

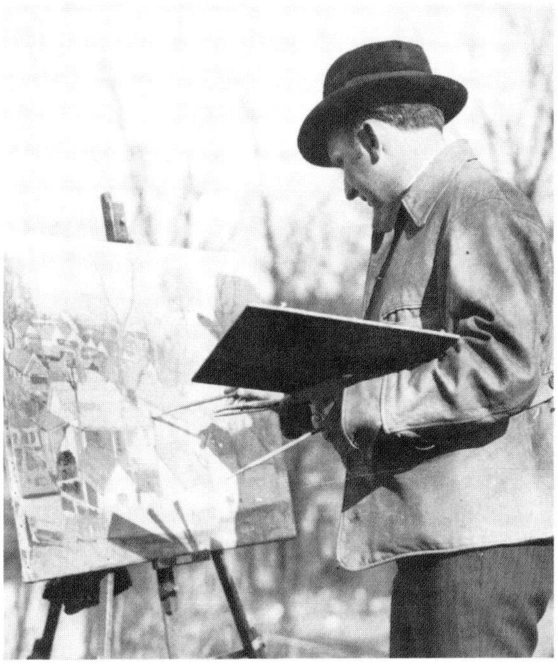

Fleck painting in Kansas City, 1923.

burned down in 1934. The Karavas brothers' Columbian Hotel (now known as La Fonda de Taos) became the new social rendezvous. Joseph A. Fleck, Jr., described some of the artists who frequented this popular gathering place:

> The waning hours of the afternoon, when the light was becoming too weak for painting, brought in the artist habitués, who made their way around the crowded tables to the back of the room where one or two booths were always reserved for them. Bisttram might have been mistaken for Tom Mix as he entered wearing a ten-gallon stetson and a neckerchief to match his shirt. Blumenschein wore a blue suit and vest, which bore evidences of recent contact with wet canvas. My father's shirt and tie combination could only have been inspired by the color scheme of one of his paintings. And Gaspard, who rode his horse to town, wore polo togs and sat with his pith helmet on the table in front of him. A chess game was usually in progress and the talk was light. Occasionally a personal quip directed across the table was followed by a burst of laughter.[1]

One of Fleck's closest and most intimate friends was the Russian-born Leon Gaspard. Since both men were of European background and spoke with strong accents, they shared common ground. Because of their foreign origins, they were sometimes treated coolly by a group of Anglos whom Gaspard called "the cream of Taos." The Flecks often spent the evening in the Gaspards' candlelit kitchen, with its Gothic windows and hand-carved wooden furniture. Much of the talk was gossip, but Gaspard often spun tales of adventure in places ranging from Taos Pueblo to faraway Mongolia.

One of the artists with whom Fleck discussed painting was Ernest L. Blumenschein. Fleck felt that some Taos painters were more illustrators than artists, but for Blumenschein, Fleck had only the highest respect. Blumenschein asserted that perseverance was the key to his own success. Undoubtedly Fleck placed an equal value on this virtue.

The year 1936 was a tragic one for the Taos art colony, due to the death of three of its prominent members. It was Fleck and Hennings who drove a stricken Walter Ufer from Taos to Santa Fe over the sinuous dirt road through the Rio Grande Gorge. Three days later, the news reached Taos that Ufer had died of a ruptured appendix in a Santa Fe hospital. That year, Taos also lost Herbert "Buck" Dunton and E. Irving Couse. Fleck was a pallbearer at both men's funerals.

Although Fleck was able to make a living by painting portraits, he decided to accept a position as Artist in Residence at the University of Kansas City (now the University of Missouri at Kansas City) in 1942. Leaving Taos was difficult for Fleck, but the University offered him other benefits. He was stimulated artistically and intellectually by the academic atmosphere. Among the many interesting contacts he made were poet John Ciardi and French author André Maurois. In 1943, Fleck was appointed to the position of Dean of the School of Fine Arts, which he held, along with his other post, until he left the university in 1946.

While at the university, Fleck became close friends with the well-known regionalist painter Thomas Hart Benton. It was Benton who inspired

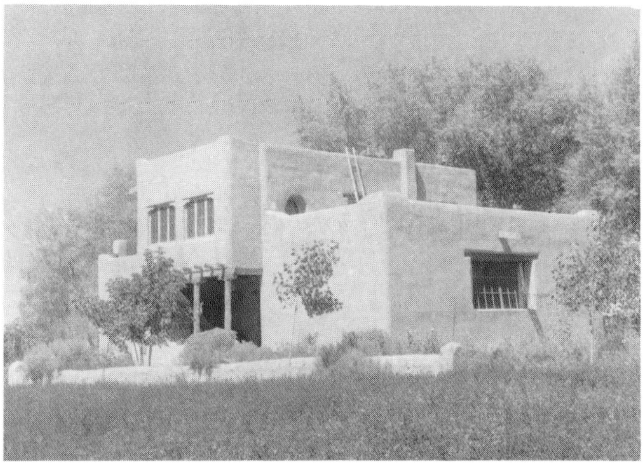

Fleck's house, which he built on La Loma, Taos, 1932.

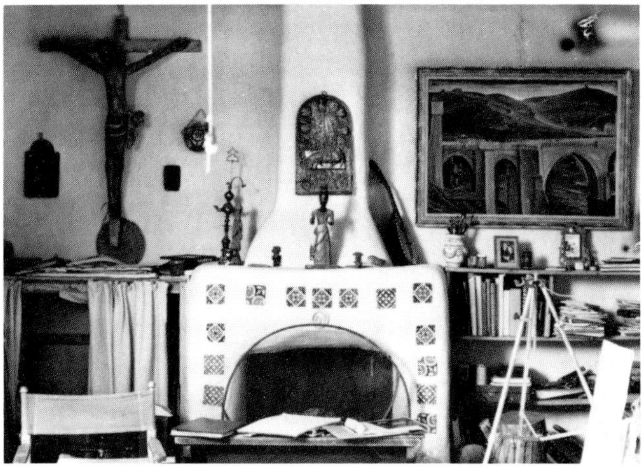

Studio in Talpa house.

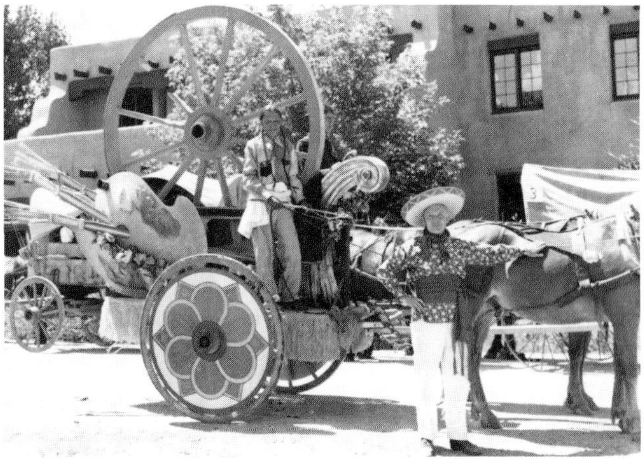

Fleck as president of the Taos Artists Association in parade, Taos, 1947.

and encouraged Fleck to continue painting in a representational way. By the 1940s, regionalism was waning, and abstract art was coming to the fore in America. Fleck spent many evenings with his mentor, who often criticized the changing art scene and the contemporary museum exhibitions, which were primarily abstract. Fleck greatly appreciated Benton's encouragement. The friendship between these two artists was to last for many years.

In the meantime, Fleck longed for New Mexico. Finally, in 1946, he decided to leave the university and return to Taos, his place of inspiration. He moved into a house in the Talpa area near Taos. His old town, he found, had changed. New artists had arrived and numerous galleries had opened. The established artists resented these changes. As a reaction, a group known as the Taos Artists Association was formed in the late 1940s. This exclusive group comprised approximately twenty-three artists who had lived and worked in Taos before 1940. All members agreed to exhibit only in La Fonda de Taos Art Gallery. Fleck presided over this organization between 1947 and 1949. The association maintained exclusive membership until the 1950s, when open membership was instituted and the name of the organization was changed to the Taos Art Association.

From the mid forties to the late sixties, Fleck continued to paint the Taos landscape and the native inhabitants, with the exception of a four-month sojourn in Portugal, where he painted a series of watercolors in fishing villages near Lisbon. Van Deren Coke wrote of Fleck's work, "By the beginning of the Forties, his firm modeling of form gave way to the use of a facile application of pigment in a style of broad impressionism. . . . In the late landscapes there was a strong emphasis on swirling smudges of bright pigment."[2] This looser style is evident in many of Fleck's later works, such as *Approaching Storm* (p. 50), which is included in this exhibition. This painting won the Grand Award, the First Prize, and the Purchase Prize for objective art in the 1965 New Mexico State Fair exhibition.

During this same period, many artists in the Taos area, including Andrew Dasburg, Cady Wells, Howard Cook, and Emil Bisttram, were

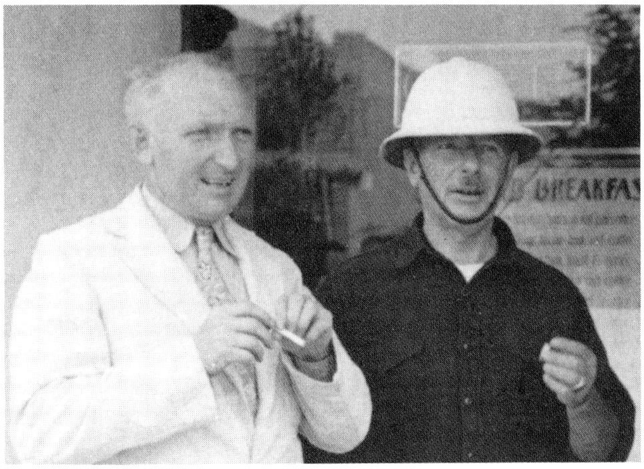
Fleck with Leon Gaspard in front of the Columbian Hotel, Taos, 1938.

incorporating modernistic devices in their painting. Fleck, in contrast, continued to go his separate way and develop his individual style. He exhibited at the Museum of Fine Arts, Museum of New Mexico, in 1954, the Oklahoma Art Center in 1949 and 1958, and the University Art Museum, University of New Mexico, where he was honored with a retrospective exhibition in 1962. In 1967, he was invited to contribute a painting to the Österreichische Galerie in Vienna's Oberes Belvedere.

Fleck's last years were difficult. In 1969, he began to experience problems with his vision. His failing eyesight forced him to stop painting in 1971. Unable to paint the golden aspens of Taos and his "flowers of the desert," the beautiful Taos Indian women, he lost all meaning in life. Mable Fleck died in 1976, and Joseph A. Fleck, one of the most important early Taos painters, died in a Pleasanton, California, nursing home on April 6, 1977.

Sandra D'Emilio
Curator of Paintings
Museum of Fine Arts, Museum of New Mexico

Footnotes

1. *Joseph A. Fleck, Jr., "Remembrances of Growing Up in the Taos Art Colony,"* Southwest Art Magazine, *June 1985, pp. 6–7.*

2. *Van Deren Coke,* Taos and Santa Fe, the Artist's Environment 1882-1942 *(Albuquerque: University of New Mexico Press, 1963), p. 67.*

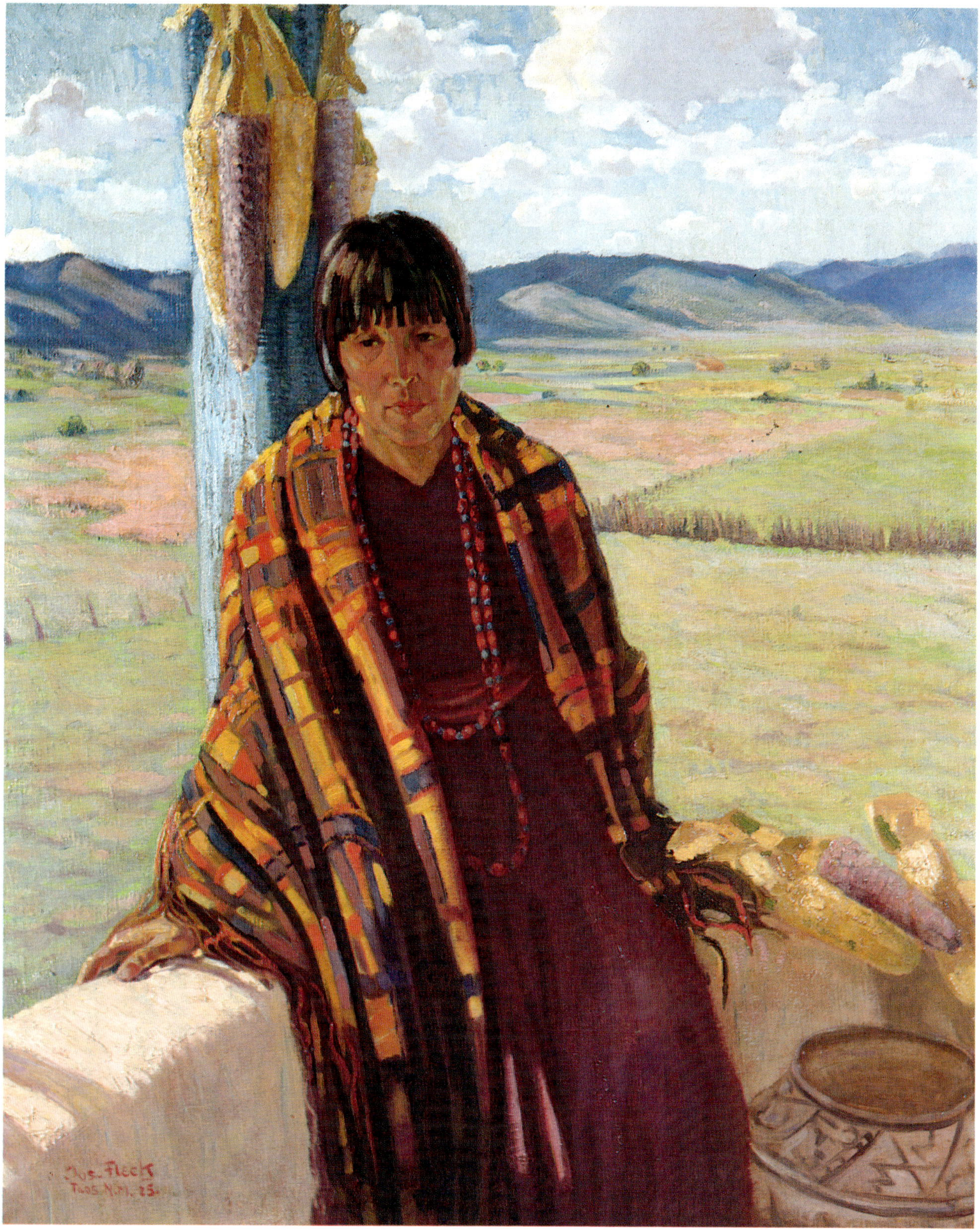

SUNNY CORNER 1925
Oil 30" x 25"
Collection of Michael J. Ross

The Paintings of Joseph A. Fleck

Joseph Fleck was a product of solid academic training in World War I era Vienna—first at the Institute for Graphic Design (program completed in 1912) and then in two sessions at the Royal Academy of Fine Arts, renamed the Vienna Academy of Fine Arts after the war (program completed with distinction in 1920). Within two years after his studies ended, he decided to emigrate to Kansas City, Missouri, partly due to the difficult economic position of Austria in the postwar period.

A brief examination of the painterly scene in Austria, notably Vienna, during Fleck's early years reveals that this artist did not fall into the highly ambitious and pictorially dramatic tradition of a Hans Makart, the social equivalent of William Merritt Chase in the United States. Nor did Fleck follow the bizarre style of an Alfred Kubin or the haunted, bravura expressiveness of an Anton Romako. Undoubtedly Fleck was aware of the increasing artistic influence of Gustav Klimt's suave art nouveau compositions with their *fin de siècle* sense of decadence and hopelessness, eating hollow the once proud Austro-Hungarian empire. It was rather to the descriptive landscapes and tranquil still lifes of Carl Schuch that Fleck inclined or to the style of Carl Moll, with its somewhat softer treatment of that real world Austria's avant-garde painters increasingly rejected. (One feels that it was as much the rise of modernism in twentieth-century Vienna as fiscal problems that led Fleck to leave his native land, where the pictorial values he esteemed were increasingly modified by formal or expressive changes.)

When Fleck arrived in Kansas City, he secured a responsible position as chief designer in a Tiffany stained-glass window workshop and was soon accepted into the social milieu of this prosperous midwestern American city. But a chance visit to a touring exhibition of the Taos Society of Artists determined his future. For most of the rest of his life, Joseph Fleck lived in Taos, with occasional periods in Kansas City—most notably from 1942 to 1946, when he was Artist in Residence at the University of Kansas City (now the University of Missouri at Kansas City) and then Dean of the School of Fine Arts.

After his marriage in 1925, Fleck returned to Europe in 1926 and again in 1930, staying into 1931. Following his second tour of Europe, when he devoted four months to painting Toledo, often in variant reflections of El Greco's earlier views of that extraordinary medieval Spanish city, Fleck exhibited at the prestigious Galerie Bernheim-Jeune in Paris with commendable press notices. His works were also shown at the Chicago Galleries Association in concert with two other American artists, Joseph Allworthy and Gerald Cassidy (another prominent southwestern painter)—with renewed press praise. However, Fleck's base remained the pueblo-style home on La Loma, its great studio facing Taos Mountain. The La Loma home, designed by Fleck and built in 1929 under his supervision by local craftsmen, was not far from the Ranchos de Taos church, which often appears in his paintings, as well as in those of many other American artists.

During Fleck's lifetime, he was widely exhibited outside of Taos and won numerous awards. Between 1924, the year of his arrival in Taos, and 1929, his paintings were shown at the Cincinnati and Milwaukee museums and the Chicago Art Institute. In 1928, he was included in both the twenty-seventh Carnegie Institute International Exhibition in Pittsburgh and the eleventh exhibition of Contemporary American Oil Paintings at the Corcoran Gallery, Washington, D.C. He exhibited in other eastern and midwestern institutions, as well as those in the Southwest, including Texas and Arizona.

After World War II, Fleck did not show in national or international exhibitions but concentrated his presentations in the Southwest—at the Oklahoma Art Center, the Museum of New Mexico at Santa Fe, and the University of New Mexico in Albuquerque, which mounted a retrospective exhibition in 1962. A special honor was the Austrian government's invitation in 1967 to contribute a 1964 landscape painting to the famous gallery of Austrian art, Österreichische Galerie in Vienna's Oberes Belvedere. Failing eyesight limited Fleck's work after 1971, and he died at Pleasanton, California, April 6, 1977.

It is interesting that virtually no graphic art and few drawings remain from an artist known during his lifetime especially for his elegant draftsmanship. From the early period, notably the two major trips to Europe, there are some vivacious and suavely descriptive Dalmatian scenes, as fresh as those of Italian artists like Italico Brass or southern California architecturally oriented painters like Elmer Grey. One of Fleck's Yugoslavian coastal town market scenes, in fact, with its high-key color scheme curiously anticipates the emphasis on hues in the Taos landscapes of the 1950s—a strange premonition of the devouring presence of sunlight in his brilliantly lighted works of later years. The Toledan scenes are more darkly brooding—in the style of El Greco or certain Austrian landscapists of the mid nineteenth century.

After Fleck's discovery of Taos, his work evolved into two major epochs of style: first the era from 1924 to about 1942, then the outpouring of incandescent landscapes after World War II. In the latter case, it was as if some youthful academic allegiance had been appeased by Fleck's immersion in academia at Kansas City from 1942 to 1946.

In Taos, the influence of the group of artists already established there was manifest in Fleck's work. The strongly bonded colony of painters was a curious outpost of American regionalism, which anticipated the artistic compartmentalization of the United States in the 1930s, as well as the Depression era's reaffirmation of realism against the rising power of European modernism. Emphasizing his personal rejection of even the wan elegance of Klimt's "Byzantine" compositions, Fleck felt immediately at home in a community much like his birthplace in the Burgenland—that agricultural province where the color of local costume and the beauty and rhythm of nature's cycles were so marked. Rather than painting the peasants of his boyhood's meeting ground between Austria and Hungary, hc turned to the Indians of Taos. Even in use of local color, he often inserted a trademark blue rebozo as part of his sitters' clothes; in composition, he made of these grave, santolike individuals a form of academic still life. Indeed, the feeling of a carefully designed still life, such as one would find in a Beaux-Arts class, invests much of his portraiture of this earlier period. He avowed that one should paint such men and women in their native setting, out-of-doors; but the fact remains that his images often show more of his handsome studio, with its views to the outside, than of the natural world itself.

Of the group who formed the original Taos Society of Artists, E. Martin Hennings had been Joseph Fleck's closest early friend. Ernest Blumenschein was also interested in Fleck, and it was with this artist that Blumenschein occasionally discussed his thoughts about painting. Inevitably, however, the European-born Fleck turned to another European in the colony, Leon Gaspard from Russia. The two families became closely knit, and while Gaspard's style had comparatively little relationship to either of Fleck's two major periods of production, the splendid color Gaspard used and the Ballet Russe-like settings he made of this New World outpost of exoticism were much admired by Fleck. Of the others, Ufer, Couse, and Dunton all died in the mid 1930s, and their fairly early removal from the community, as well as the economic problems of the Great Depression, certainly affected Fleck. While the artist had his own firm concept of realism, there are special resonances between his work and that of Ernest Blumenschein or the older Joseph Henry Sharp, especially in their Indian genre portraits. (There seems to have been some affinity between Fleck and the native people of the area, whether Indian or Spanish-American.) In Fleck's later landscapes, echoes of Hennings and Ufer appear.

Since Joseph Fleck was a painter of numerous commissioned portraits, his works of this type are widely scattered among the homes of his clients or their descendants. Few of such works are included in the present exhibition. However, the fine portrait of his wife, Mable Mantz Fleck, indicates the type. In almost all of his portrait studies, Fleck favored a three-quarter figure, usually placed at an angle in the left or right corner of his composition. There are some charmingly fresh head studies of young girls and one especially lively and spontaneous *esquisse* of his son, Joseph A. Fleck, Jr., which emphasizes the head. But even in this latter work, as well as those of the girls, the face is turned a quarter left or right to reveal the full character of the features. One strong Indian work, *Flying Cloud* (p. 31), is close to a profile; here one sees that Fleck felt the glyptic power of the bronzed face and assertive nose were more important than the revelation of social personality, a major concern in his more official portraits. Fleck was inclined to paint musicians, whether a crouching cellist who embraces his large instrument with sinuous curvilinear rhythms, a lone mature guitarist with a telling vignette of the Ranchos church, or a more youthful pair of musicians gazing intently forward (another Fleck device in certain portraits to connect sitter and viewer). Some of his subjects are closely linked with objects of their crafts, as in *Pottery Girl* (p. 29) or *Mexican Bottler* (p. 20). The work that most tellingly sums up Fleck's portrait work is *Fiesta Array* (cover), in which three native women are grouped at the left and right foreground of a spreading landscape, with the town in the center. The single woman at the left holds a *santo de bulto,* which emphasizes her own ritualistic stance. A younger woman or girl at the right holds a fine pottery bowl, while a more enigmatic woman turns her body and face away from the painter and wears Fleck's archetypical blue and white rebozo. In all these portraits, a stasis, or calm dignity of pose, is basic. There is little emotion in Fleck's portraits (unlike those of his Austrian contemporary Oskar Kokoschka); they belong to a special realm of suspended time and are more icons than human dramas.

After his return in 1946 from Kansas City, where he had become a close friend of Thomas Hart Benton, Joseph Fleck increasingly turned to landscape. As has been noted, many of his portraits of the 1930s had been commissioned works, which place psychological and personal limitations on artists. Like John Singer Sargent, Fleck repudiated the tedious exactions of prosperous or ego-oriented persons who wanted their personae immortalized; he began a highly productive love affair with landscape. Like the eastern painter Charles Burchfield, Fleck was literally consumed by the essence of local natural forces. The rolling terrain of the Taos valley and its ring of nearby mountains, the towering cottonwoods, and the dry bushes are eroded into flickering flames of sunstruck brilliance. With the cubic forms of the adobe buildings that are the principal architectural structures of the area and the massive buttresses and lofty towers of that leitmotif of the community—the church at Ranchos de Taos—Fleck weaves a hundred variations on this productive but semiarid country. Almost all the paintings have wide horizontal formats, emulating the spreading valley of Taos and its immense skies. His range changes palpably from the rather solid colors of the earlier period to a high-key palette of yellow, orange, red, and intense blue. This was the era when more members of the Taos Society of Artists were dying—Berninghaus in 1952, Hennings in 1956, and Blumenschein in 1960. Fleck became possessed of a will to paint that literally exploded in his numerous works of the 1950s.

The portraits had been either smoothly brushed and contoured in a thoughtfully academic manner or sometimes more prismatically painted with multiple surface facets. The landscapes mirror a much more complex approach to subject and technique; they often verge on a form of spiritual expressionism not unlike the late work of Vlaminck. Some of Fleck's landscapes show a kind of quiet regional structuralism, derived from local mountain forms or adobe building shapes and allied in a very general way to Cézanne and the Cubists, thus paralleling the New Mexican work of J. Ward Lockwood or slightly echoing ideas of John Marin. Examples are Fleck's *Early Spring in Llano,* (p. 55) and *Vista of Rain* (p. 51). A number of Fleck's landscapes, such as *Summer Day* (p. 46) or *New Mexico Landscape* (p. 53), have an almost thirtyish rural character, allied to the works of Benton.

Gradually a compelling vitalism invests land and sky. Trees rise like eternal pyres to an abundance of clouds, which take on the mutable form of primordial matter, regrouping themselves in abstract patterns as in the dawn of creation. Avenues of enormous trees, as in *Going Home, Summer* (p. 43) and *Going Home, Autumn* (p. 42), become metaphors of landscape's self-consumption in the destructive cycles of the year—matter devouring itself in a frenzy of eternal seasonal change.

A new formula for painting is apparent, one in which light washes and small, intense strokes of oil conjure up the delicacy and fervor of aspiring branches and leaves. The iconic quiet of Fleck's portraits turns into a supernal immolation of nature that verges on lyric poetry. To put it in musical terms, the solemn plainsong of the portraits becomes a Wagnerian psychodrama in which nature's creations are the passionate singers of their personal ecstasy.

Joseph Amadeus Fleck has been incompletely viewed in the past. His earlier career revolved around solidly painted commissioned portraits and studies of people in his beloved Taos. These earlier paintings and the later landscapes each reached appreciative audiences in their times. The present exhibition provides a more adequate interpretation of the variety and fullness of Fleck's accomplishments.

European born and educated, like many other twentieth-century "American" artists, Fleck successfully effected the difficult transfer from Old World to New World life. Colorfully dressed in his own inimitable manner, the outspoken Fleck was a much-admired member of the Taos colony. More than any other artist in the original group, he lived to see the profound changes in that unique place of constant artistic interchange and intense accomplishment. Gifted with a zest that matched the dry intensity of the site, his work evolved from the quiet formality of his portraits to the spontaneous fervor of his landscapes. Always a fine and exacting technician, Joseph Fleck achieved a personal growth that places him in a special position at this crossroads of American art.

Joseph Armstrong Baird, Jr.
Professor of Art History
University of California, Davis

Paintings in the Joseph A. Fleck Traveling Exhibition

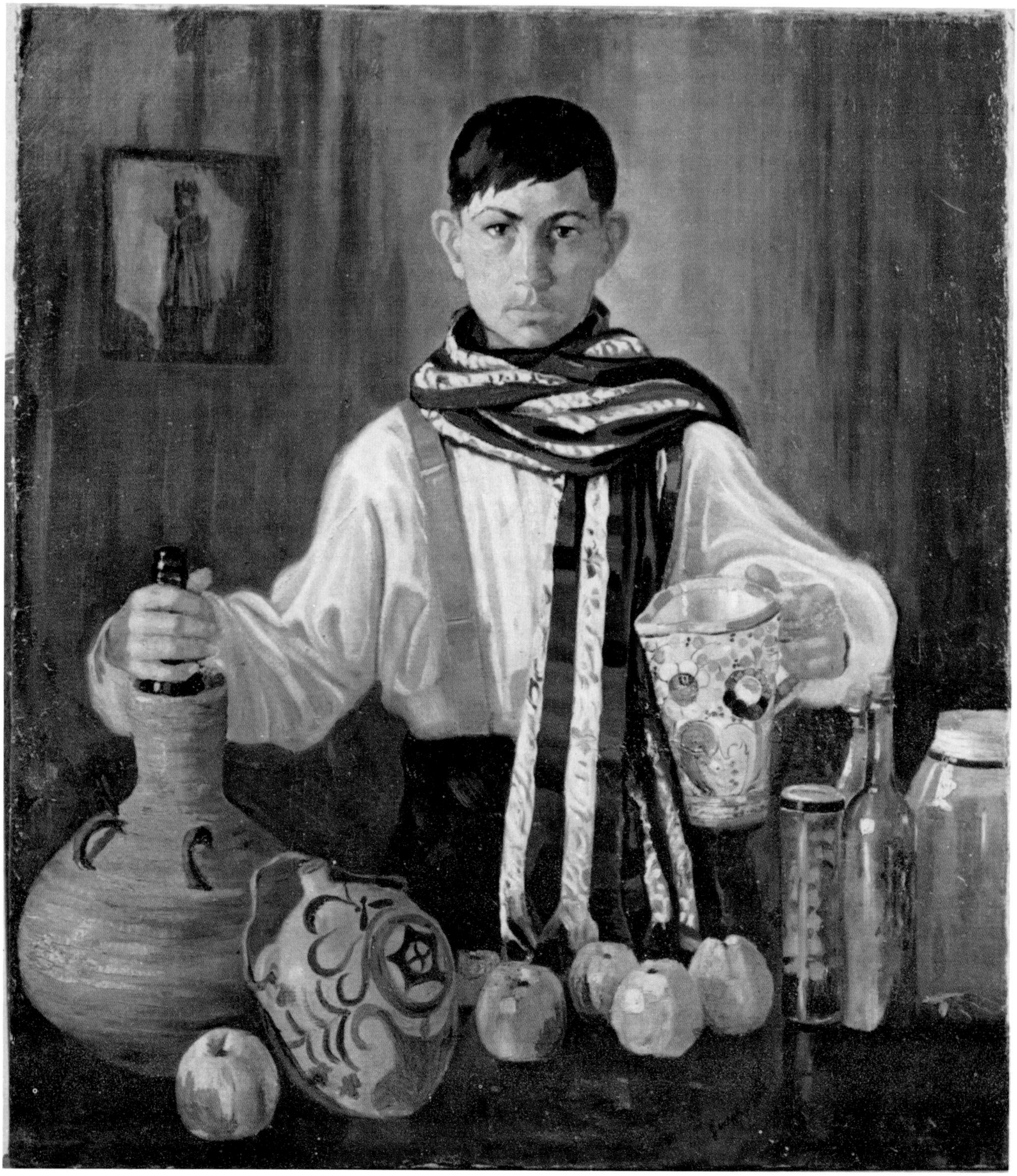

MEXICAN BOTTLER 1926
Oil 33" x 29"
Collection of Joseph A. Fleck, Jr.

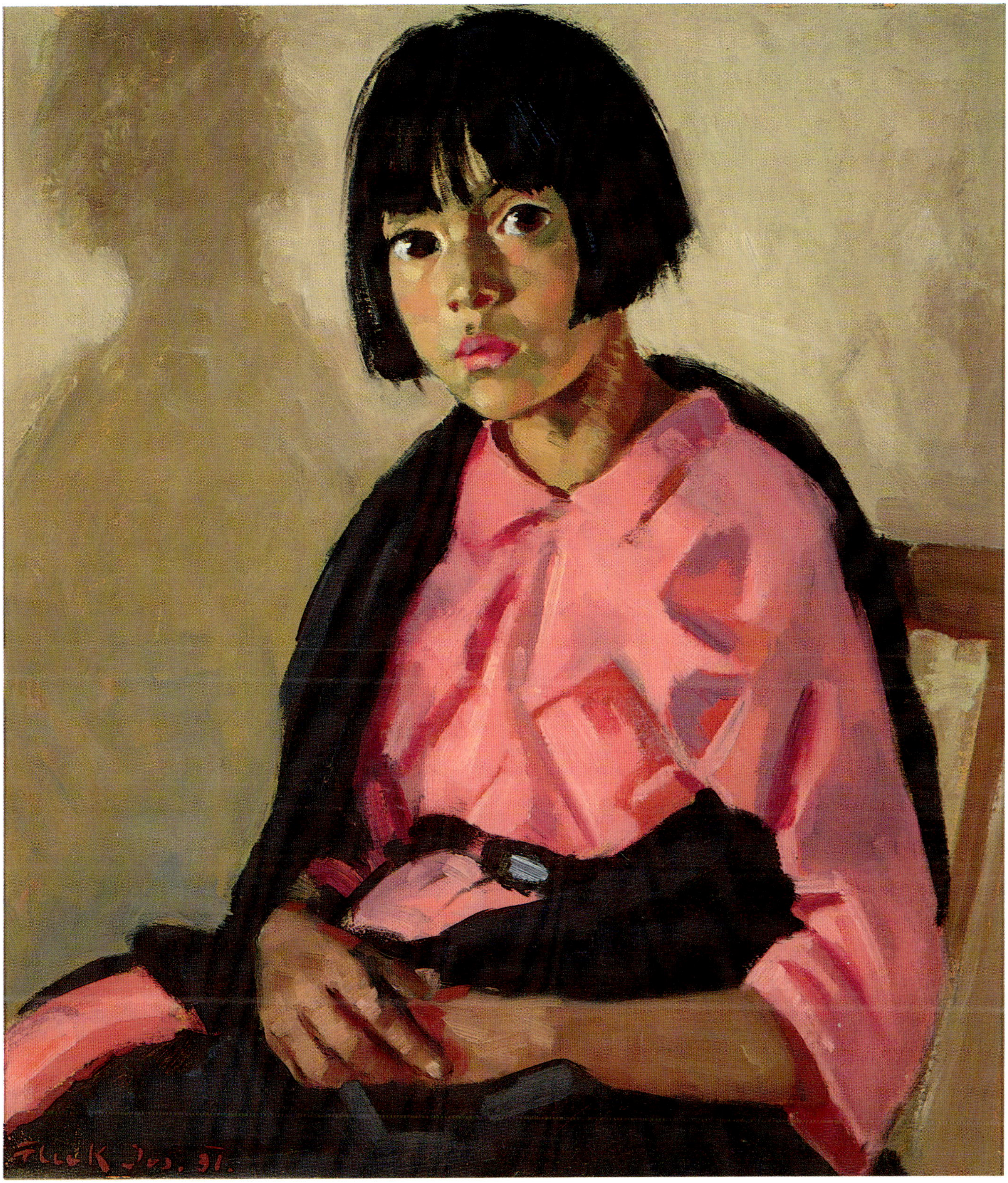

ROSITA 1931
Oil 18" x 17¼"
The Nelson-Atkins Museum of Art, gift from the Howard P. Treadway and Tertia F. Treadway Collection

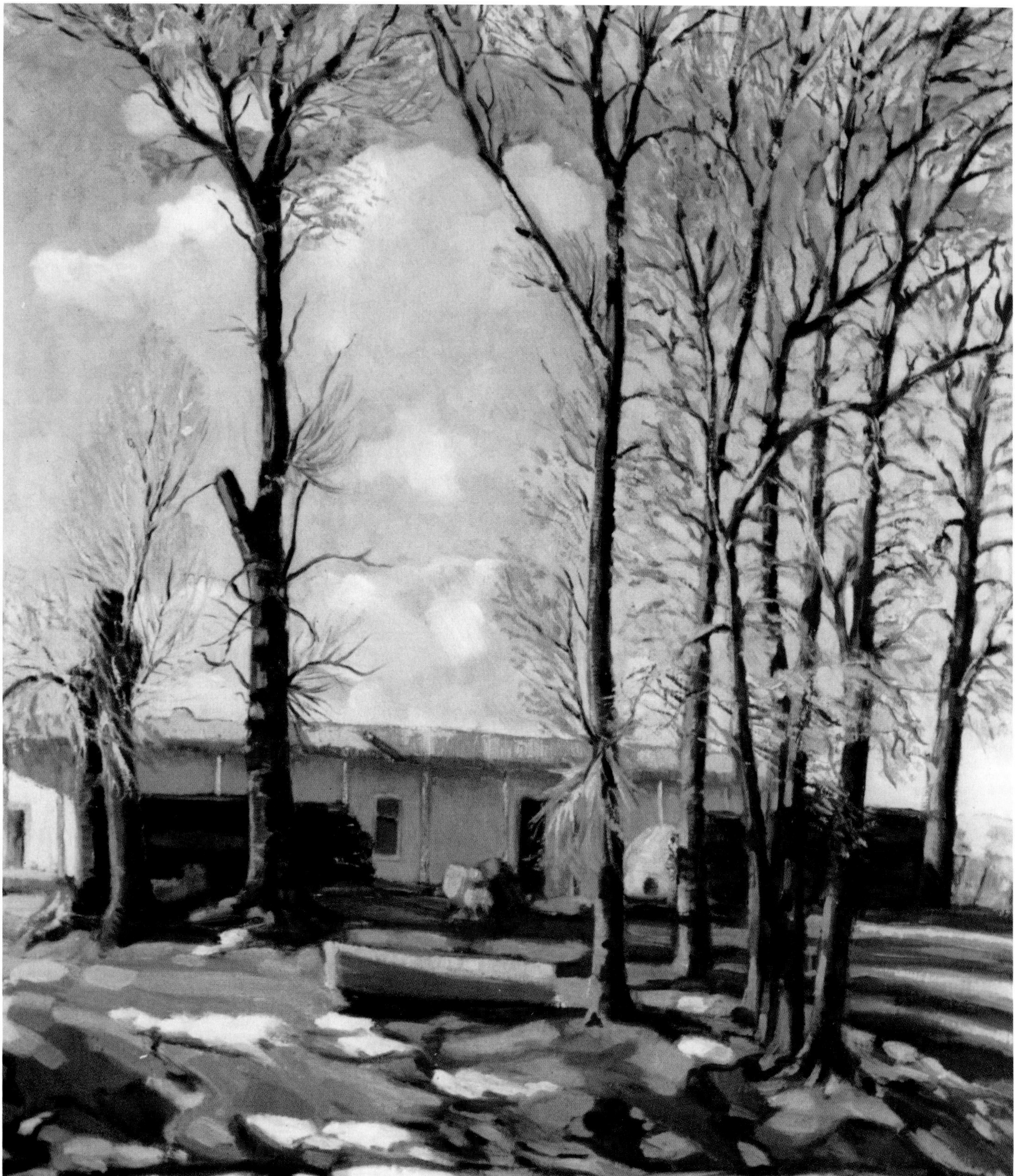

OLD SPANISH HOME 1925
Oil 24" x 27"
Collection of the El Paso Museum of Art

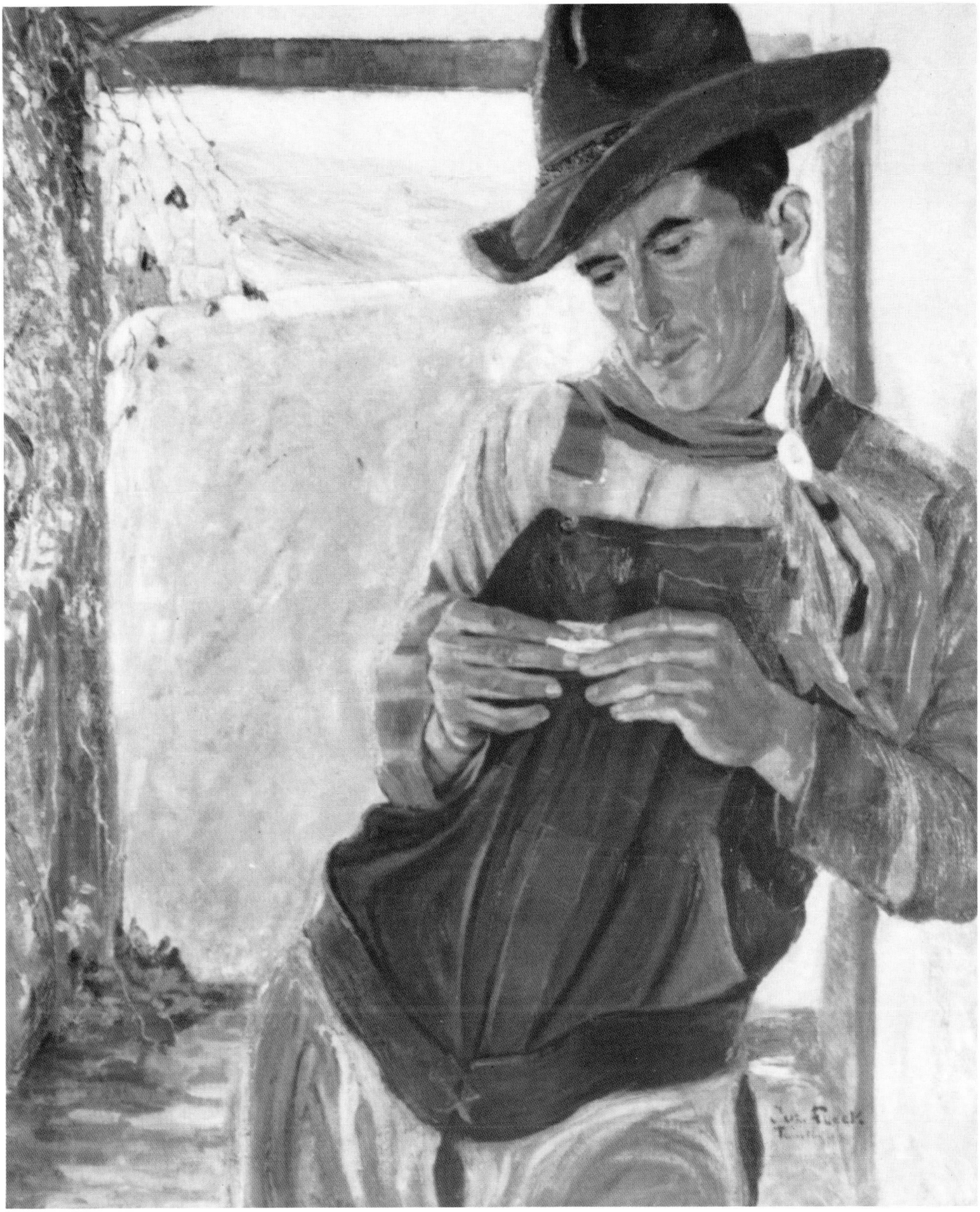

SPANISH COWBOY 1925
Oil 25" x 30"
Collection of Western Art and Artifacts of
Business Men's Assurance Company of America

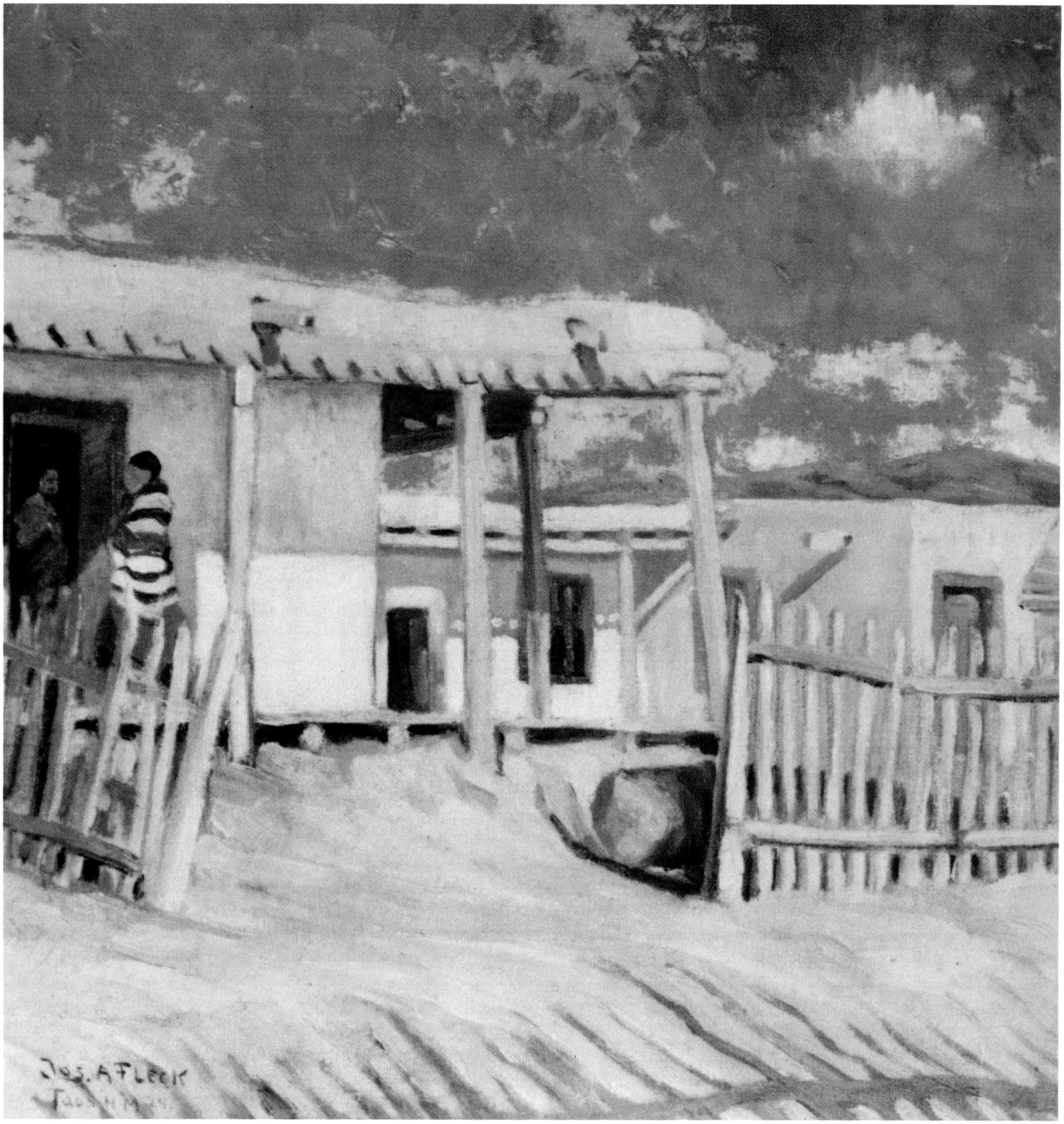

HOUSE IN THE SUN 1924
Oil 13⅝" x 13⅝"
Collection of Mr. and Mrs. Robert E. McKee III

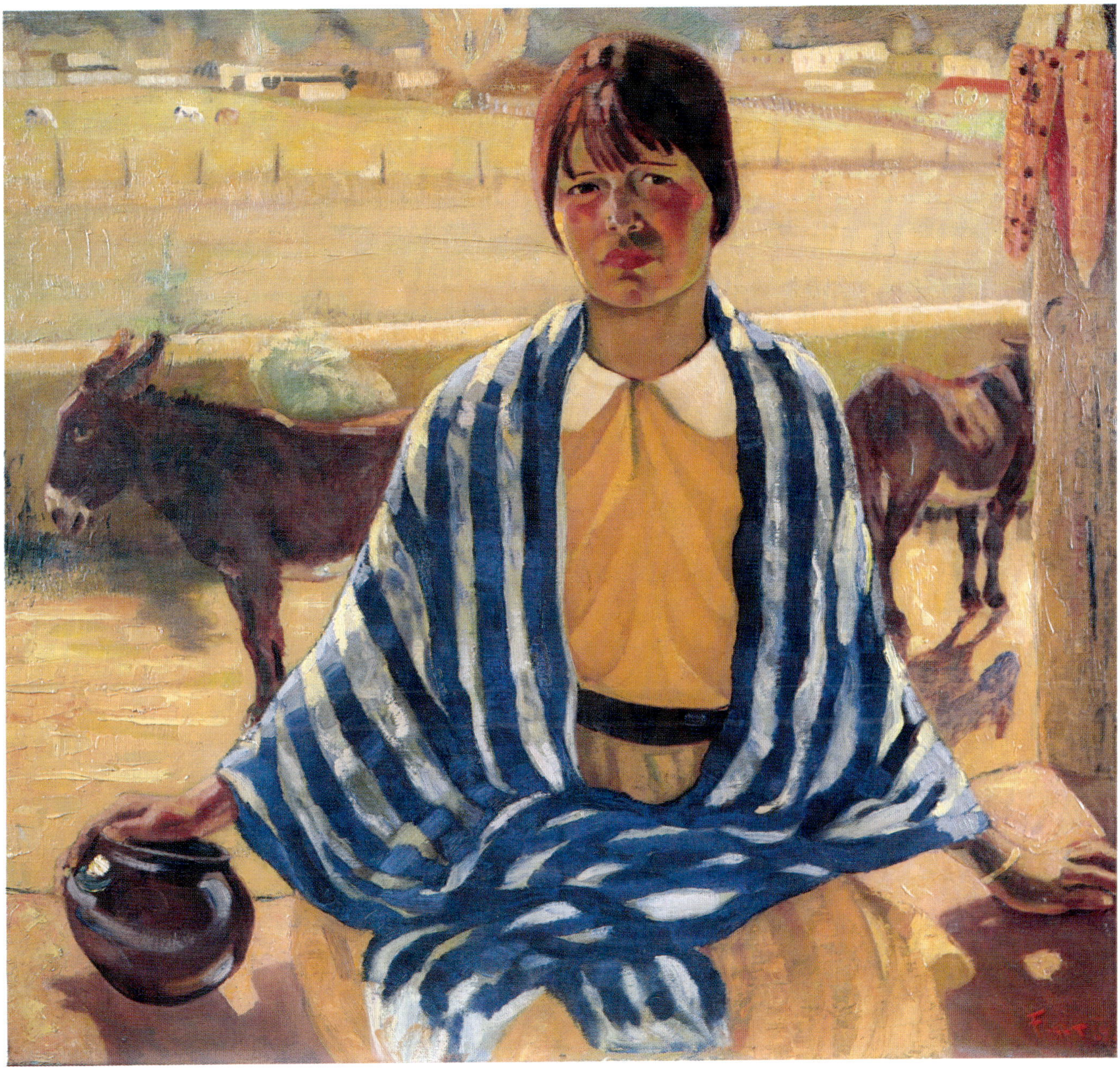

INDIAN SUMMER 1929
Oil 32½" x 35¼"
Collection of Mr. and Mrs. Joseph Szymanski

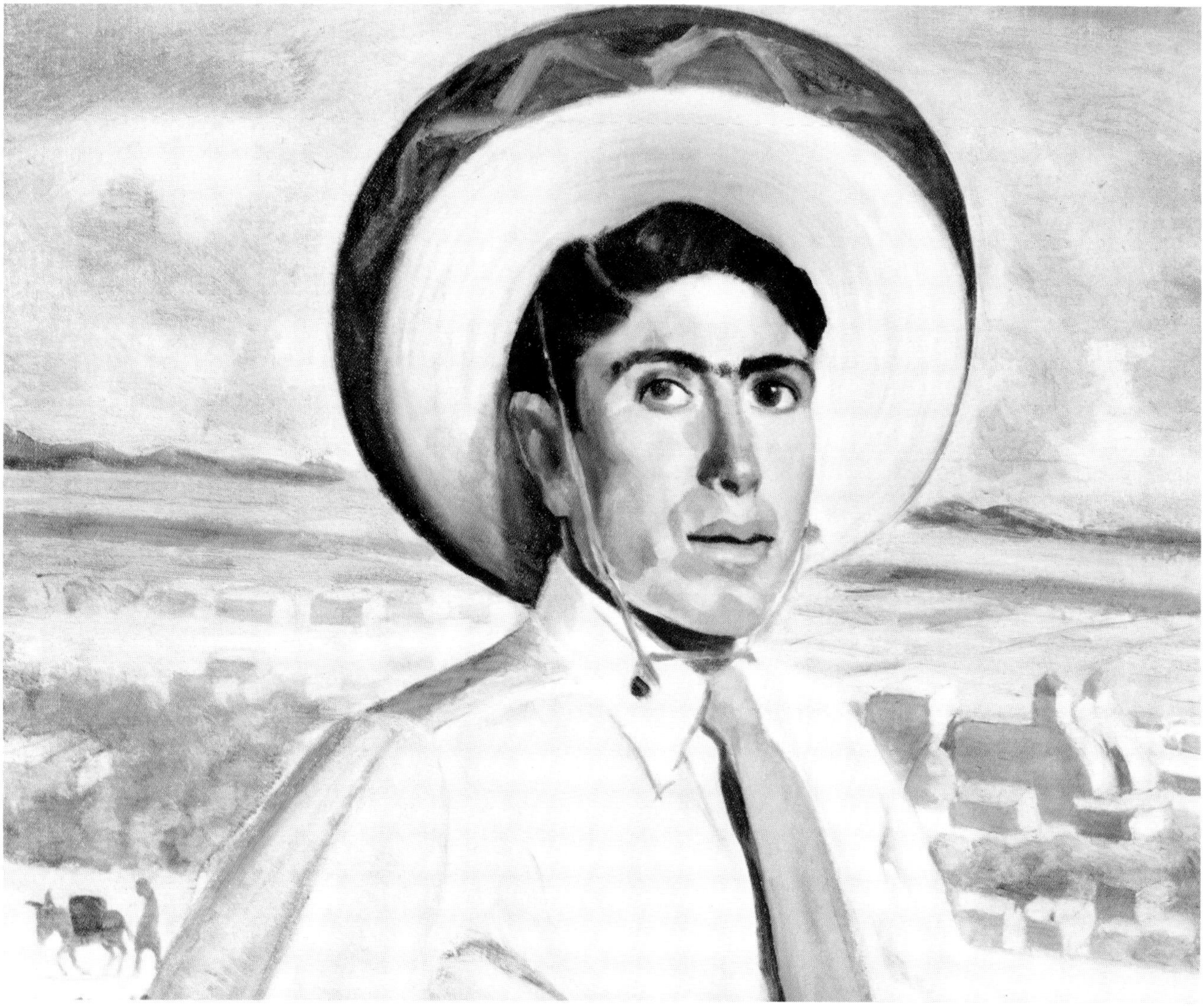

YOUNG MAN WITH SOMBRERO 1931
Oil 20" x 24"
Collection of Joseph A. Fleck, Jr.

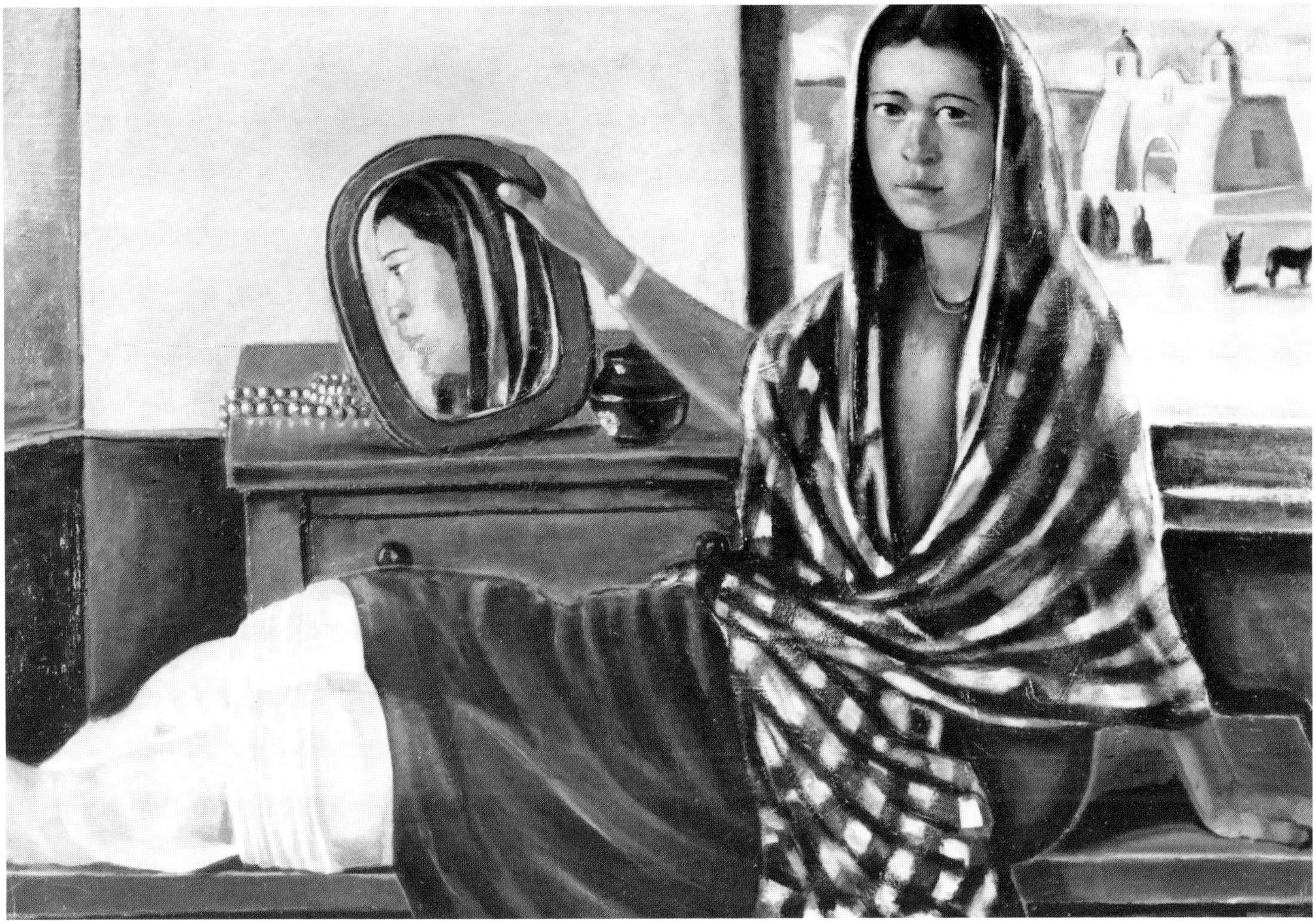

INDIAN BRIDE 1935
Oil 31" x 45"
Collection of Joseph A. Fleck, Jr.

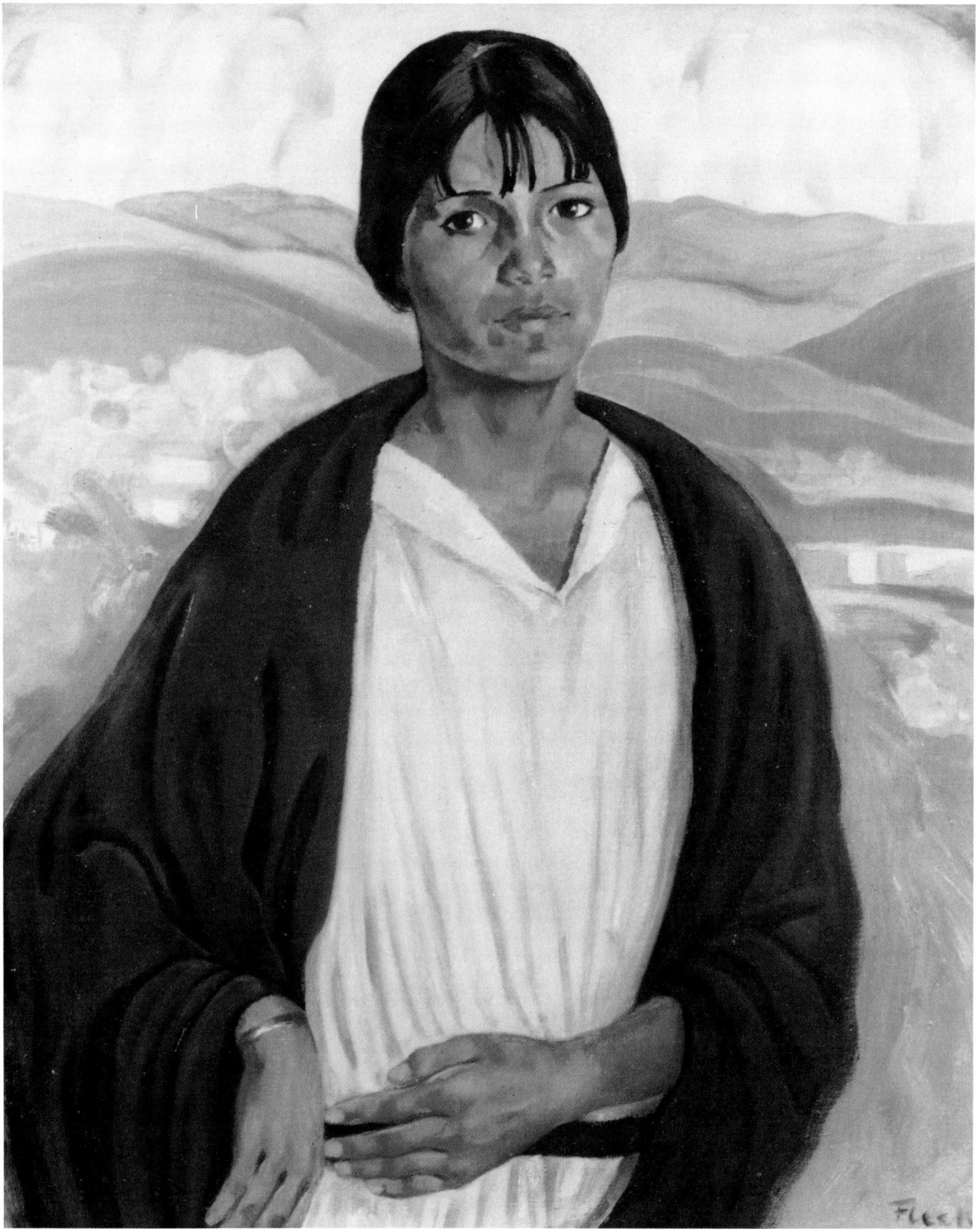

AMARILLA 1930
Oil 30" x 25"
The Carl and Elisabeth Waldo Dentzel Collection

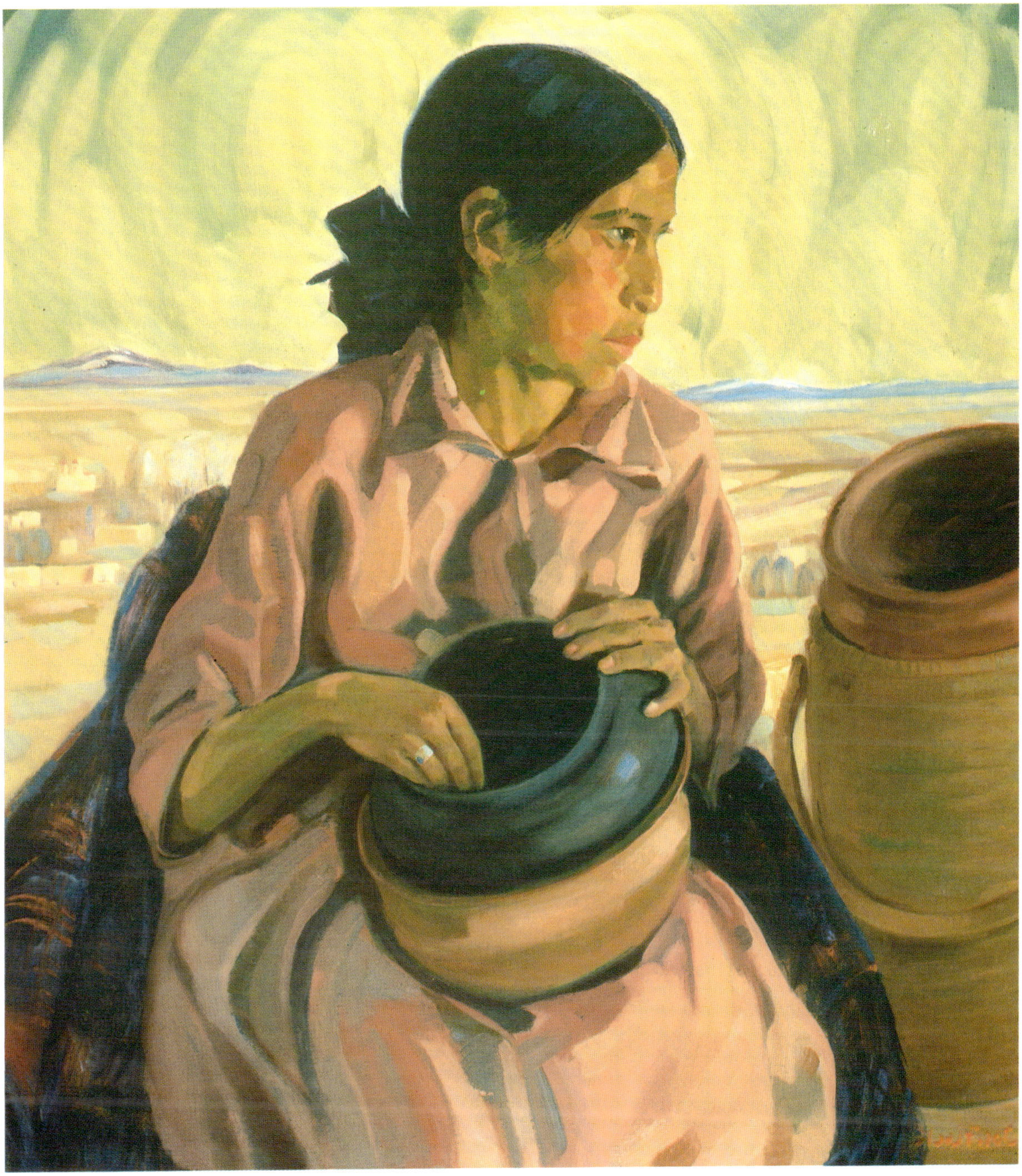

POTTERY GIRL 1929
Oil 31" x 27½"
Collection of Mr. and Mrs. Robert E. McKee III

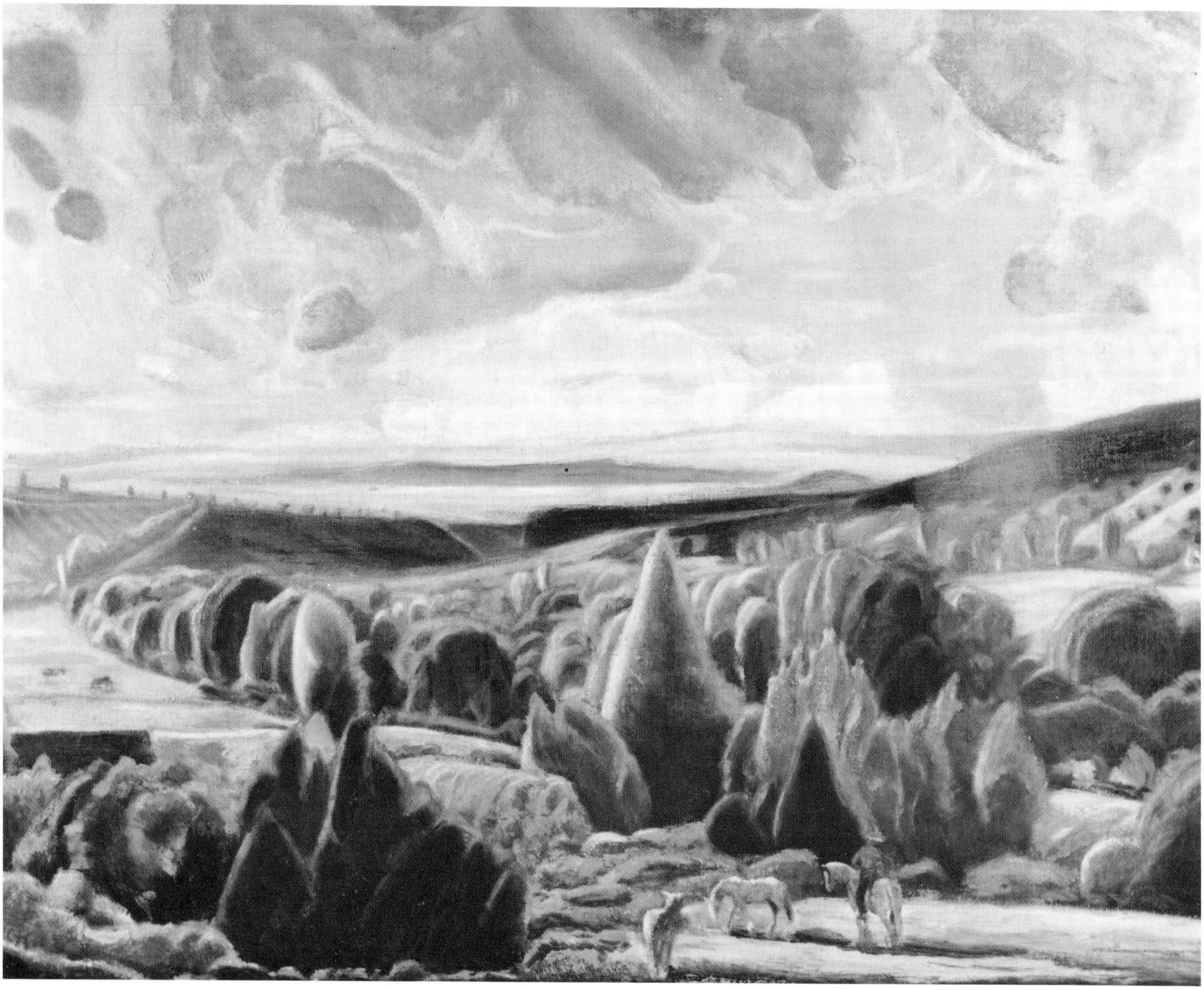
HONDO CANYON, LOOKING WEST 1938
Oil 24" x 32"
Collection of Michael J. Ross

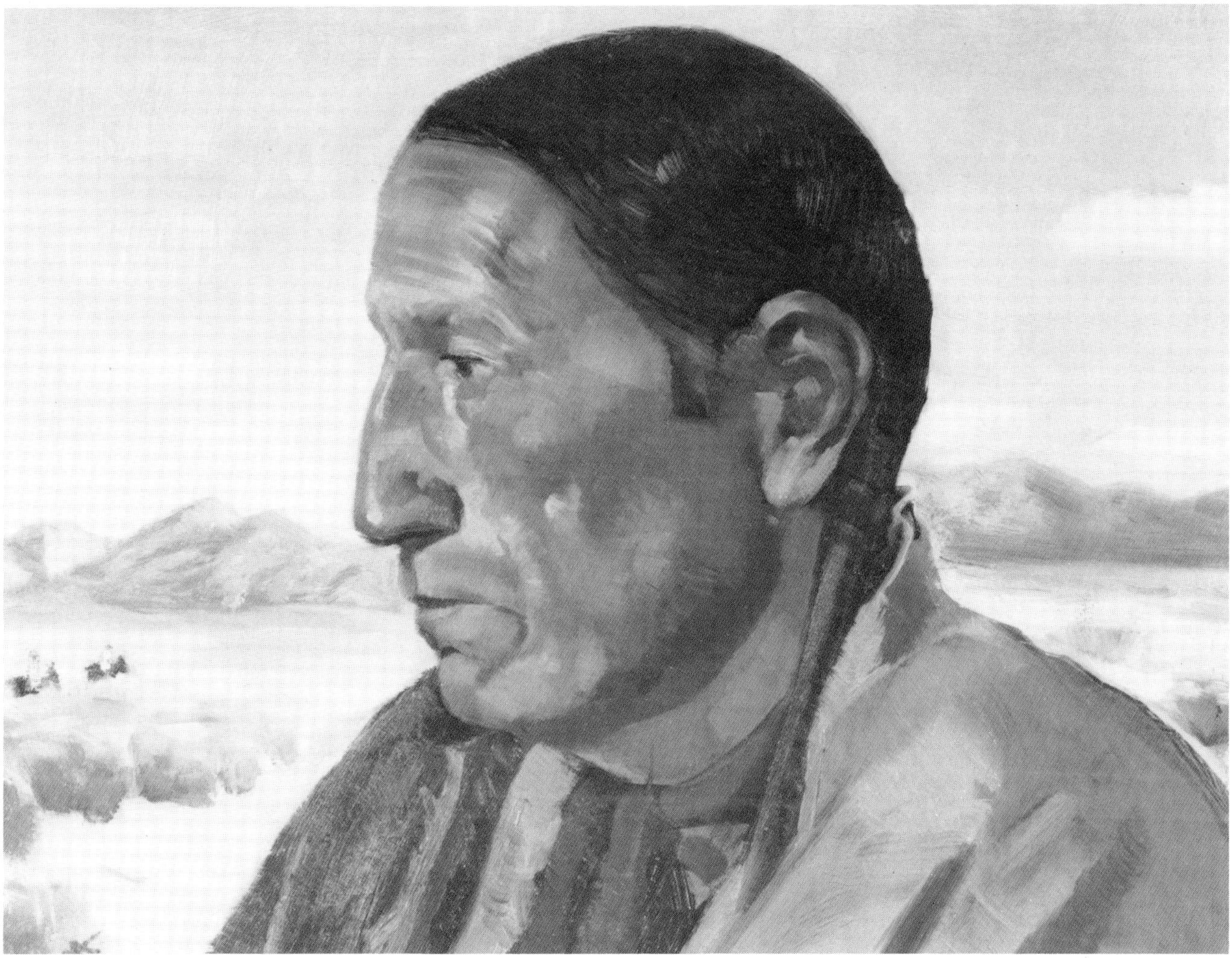

FLYING CLOUD 1934
Oil 12" x 16"
Collection of Joseph A. Fleck, Jr.

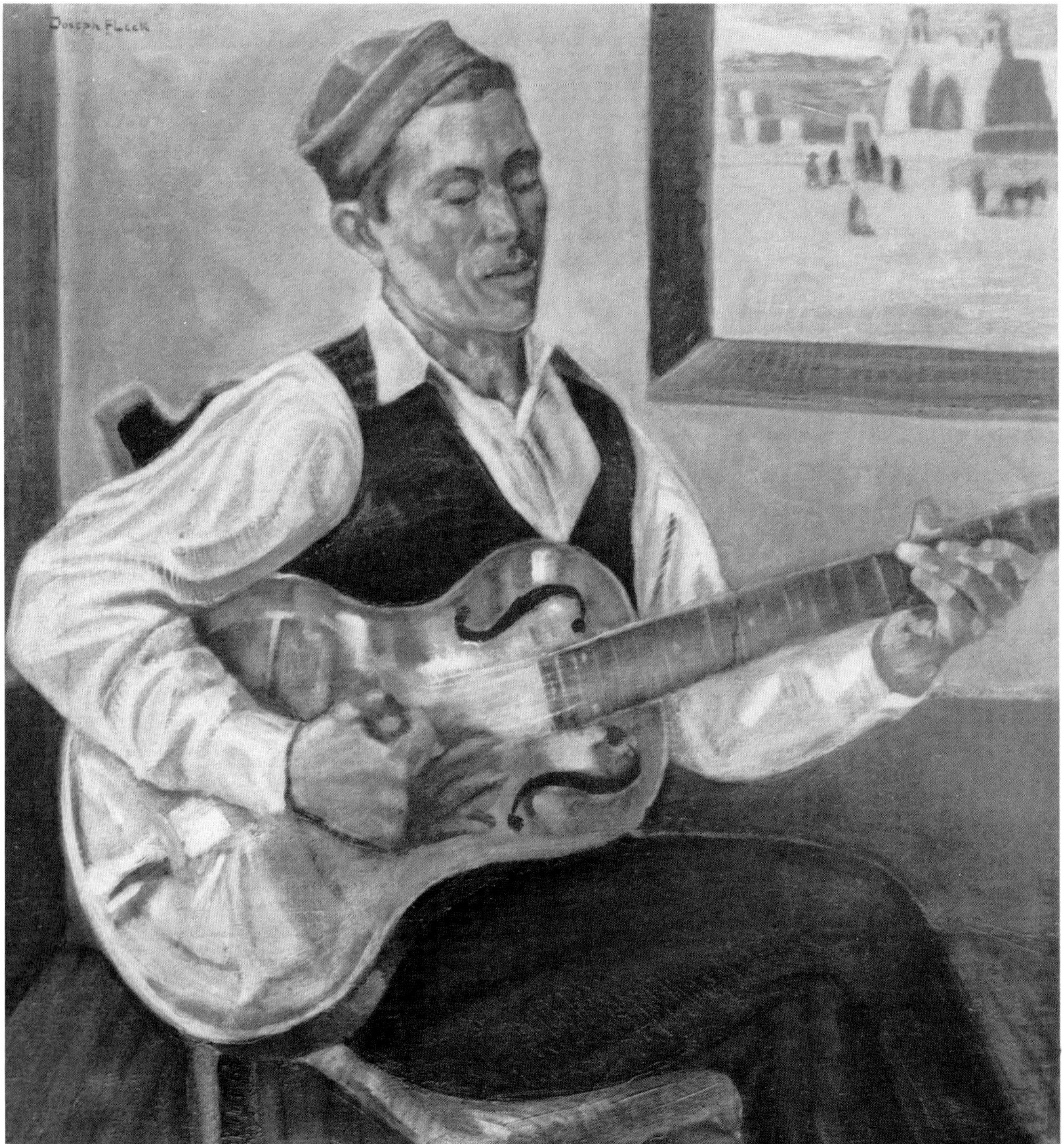

THE GUITARIST 1938
Oil 35⅛" x 32"
Collection of the Museum of Fine Arts, Museum of New Mexico

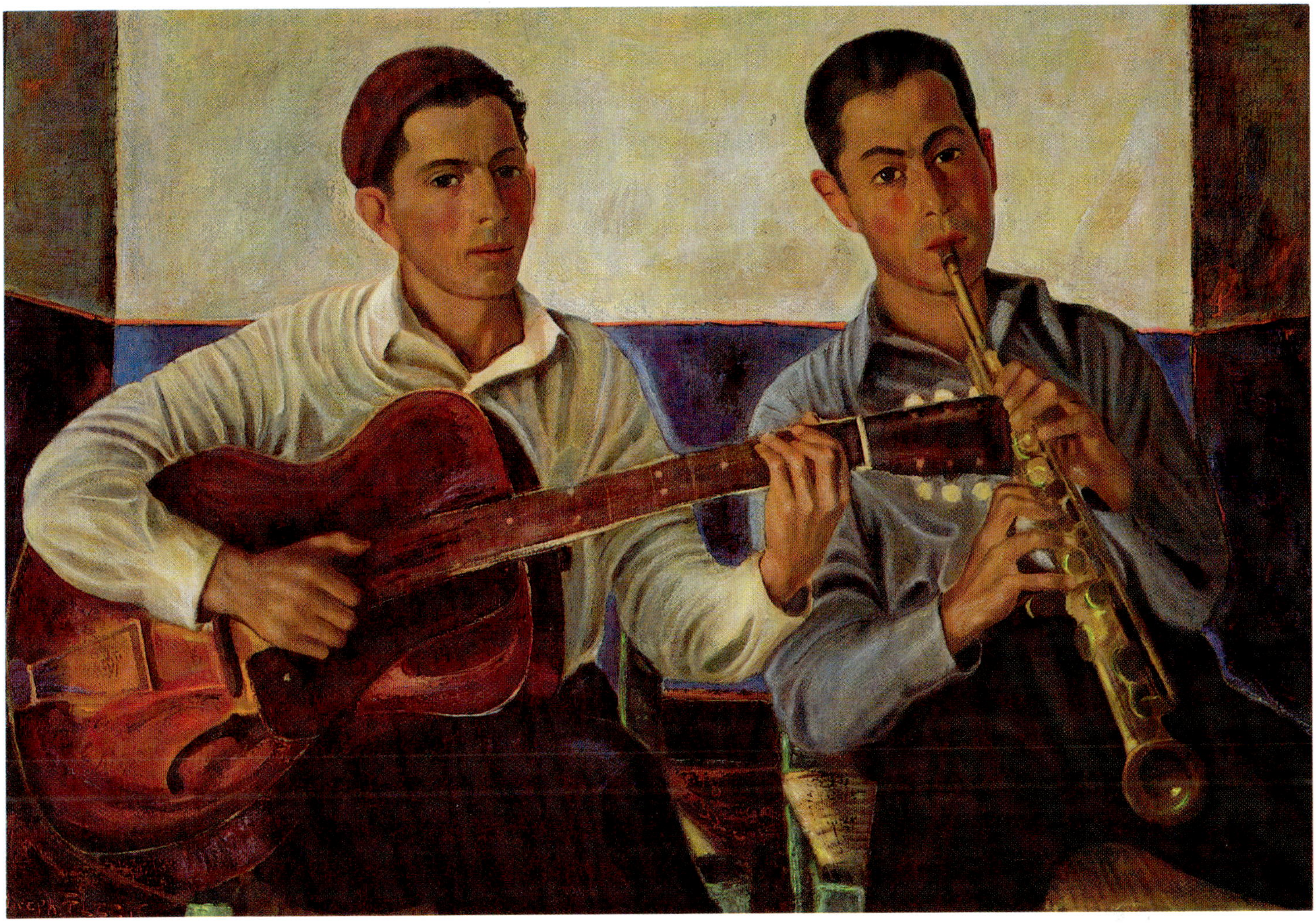

TWO SPANISH MUSICIANS 1938
Oil 30¼" x 43¾"
Collection of the University Art Museum,
University of New Mexico

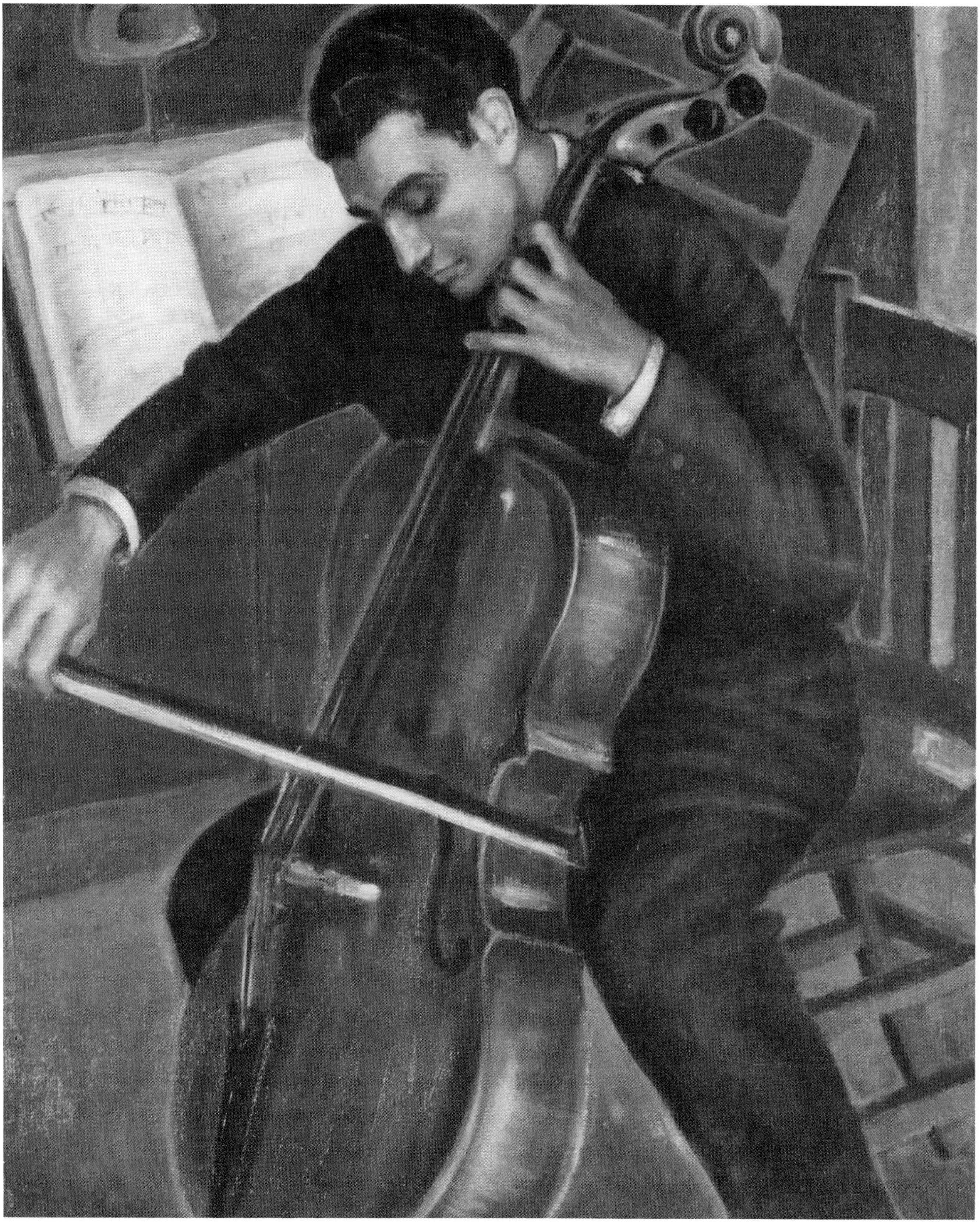

THE CELLO PLAYER 1944
Oil 30" x 25"
Collection of Joseph A. Fleck, Jr.

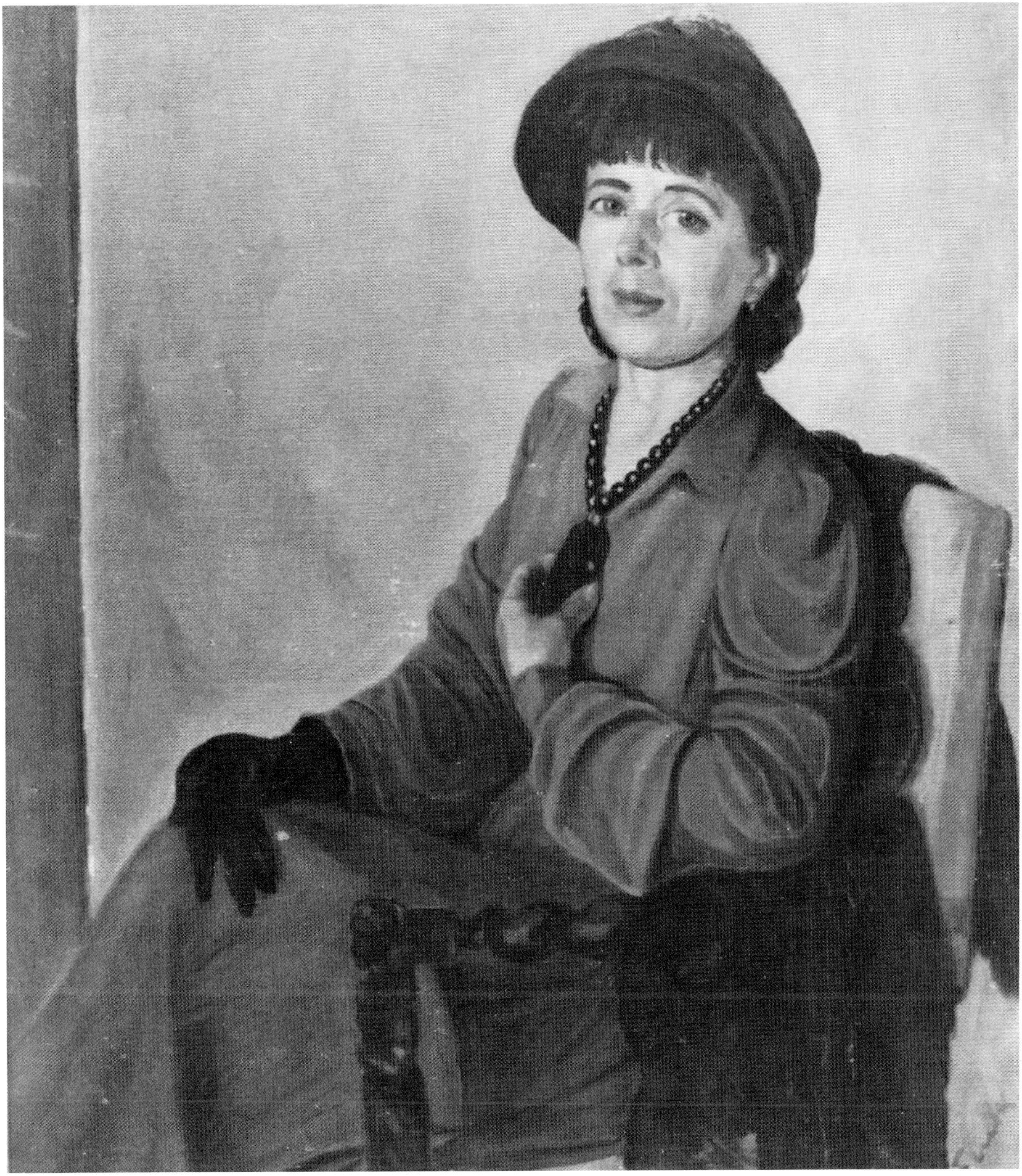

PORTRAIT OF NOULA 1938
Oil 32" x 27"
Collection of The Harwood Foundation Museum
of Taos Art

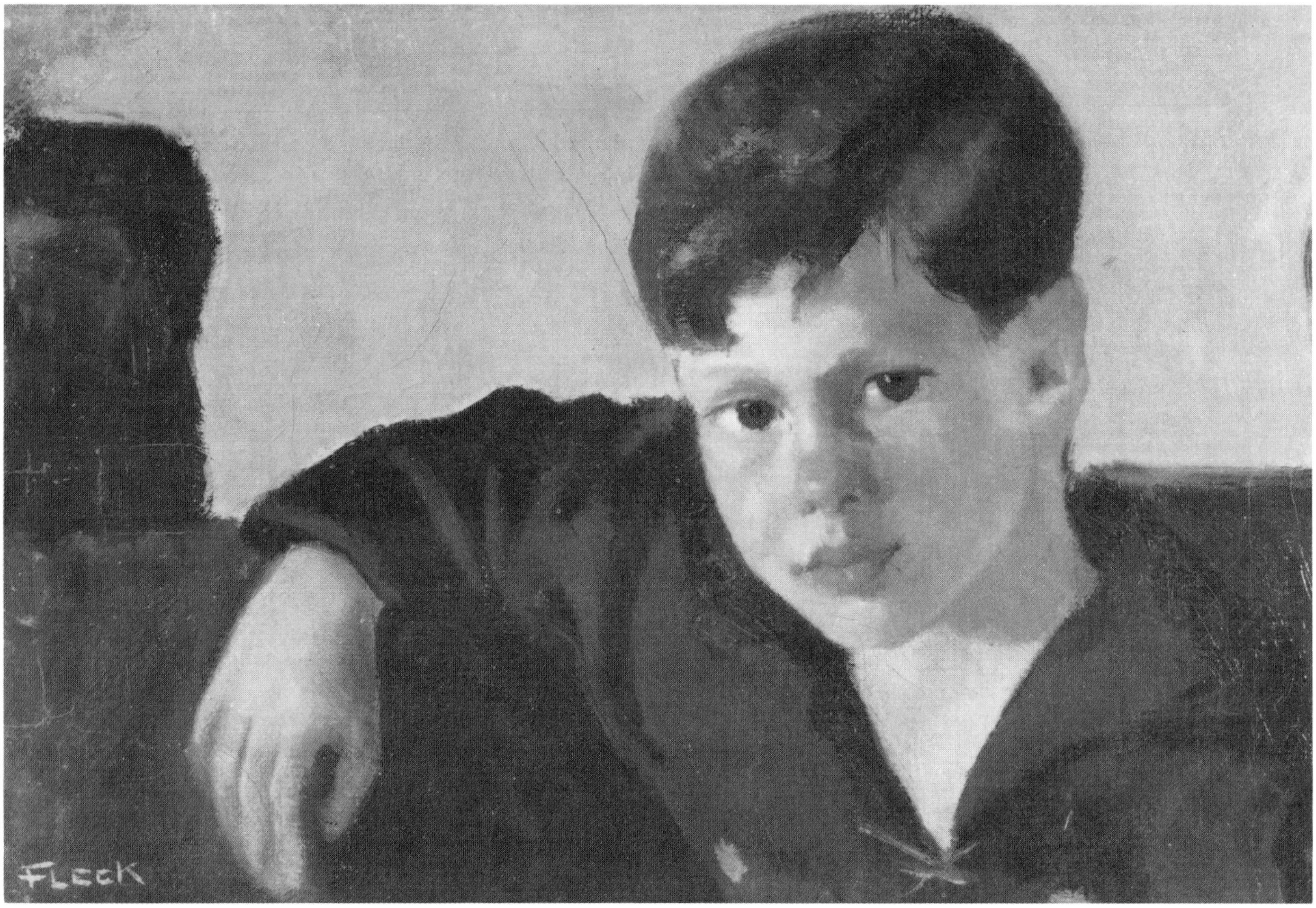

PORTRAIT OF THE ARTIST'S SON 1932
Oil 12" x 18"
Collection of Joseph A. Fleck, Jr.

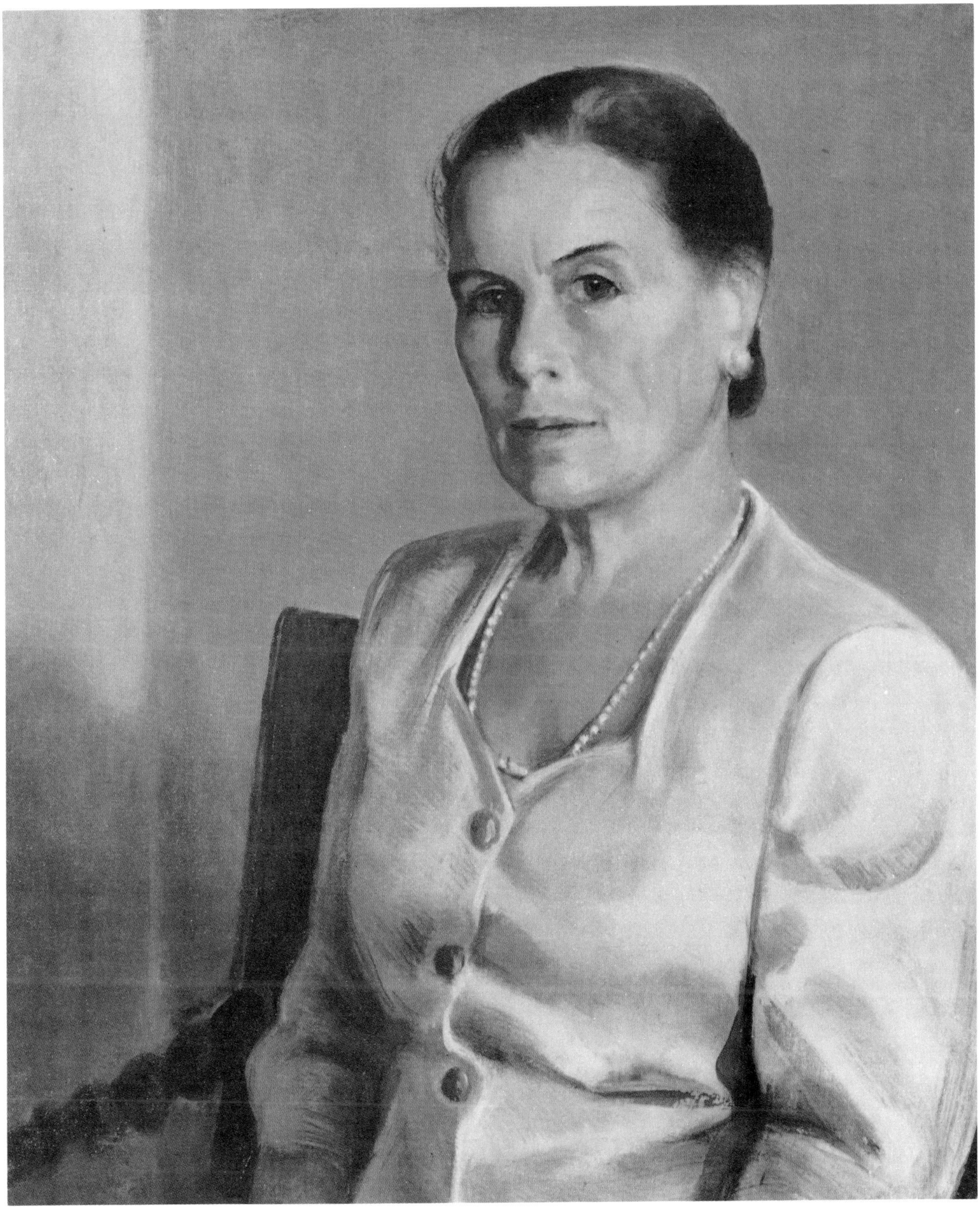

PORTRAIT OF THE ARTIST'S WIFE 1951
Oil 20" x 24"
Collection of Joseph A. Fleck, Jr.

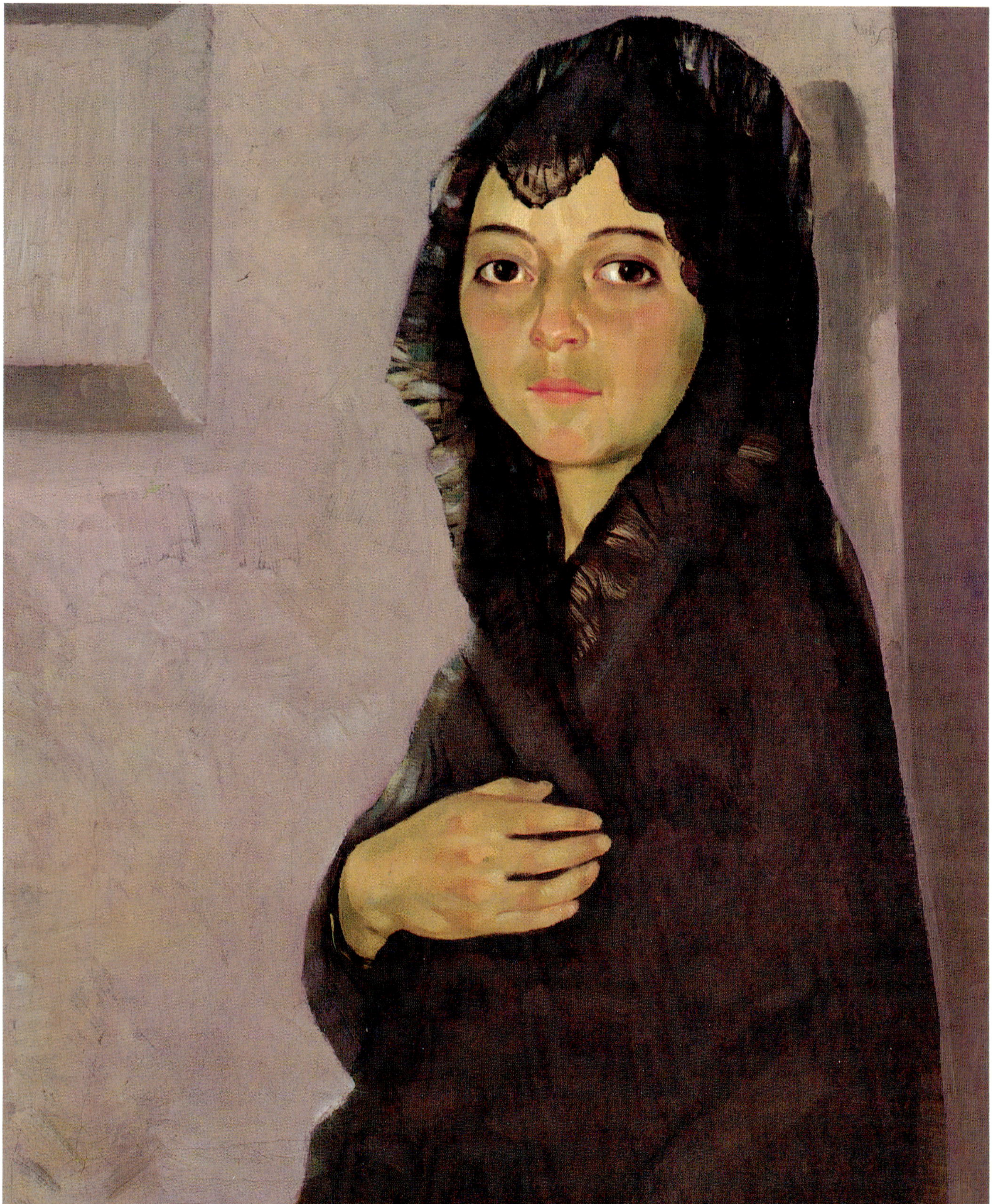

GIRL WITH MANTILLA 1933
Oil 24" x 20"
Collection of Lewis L. Dail

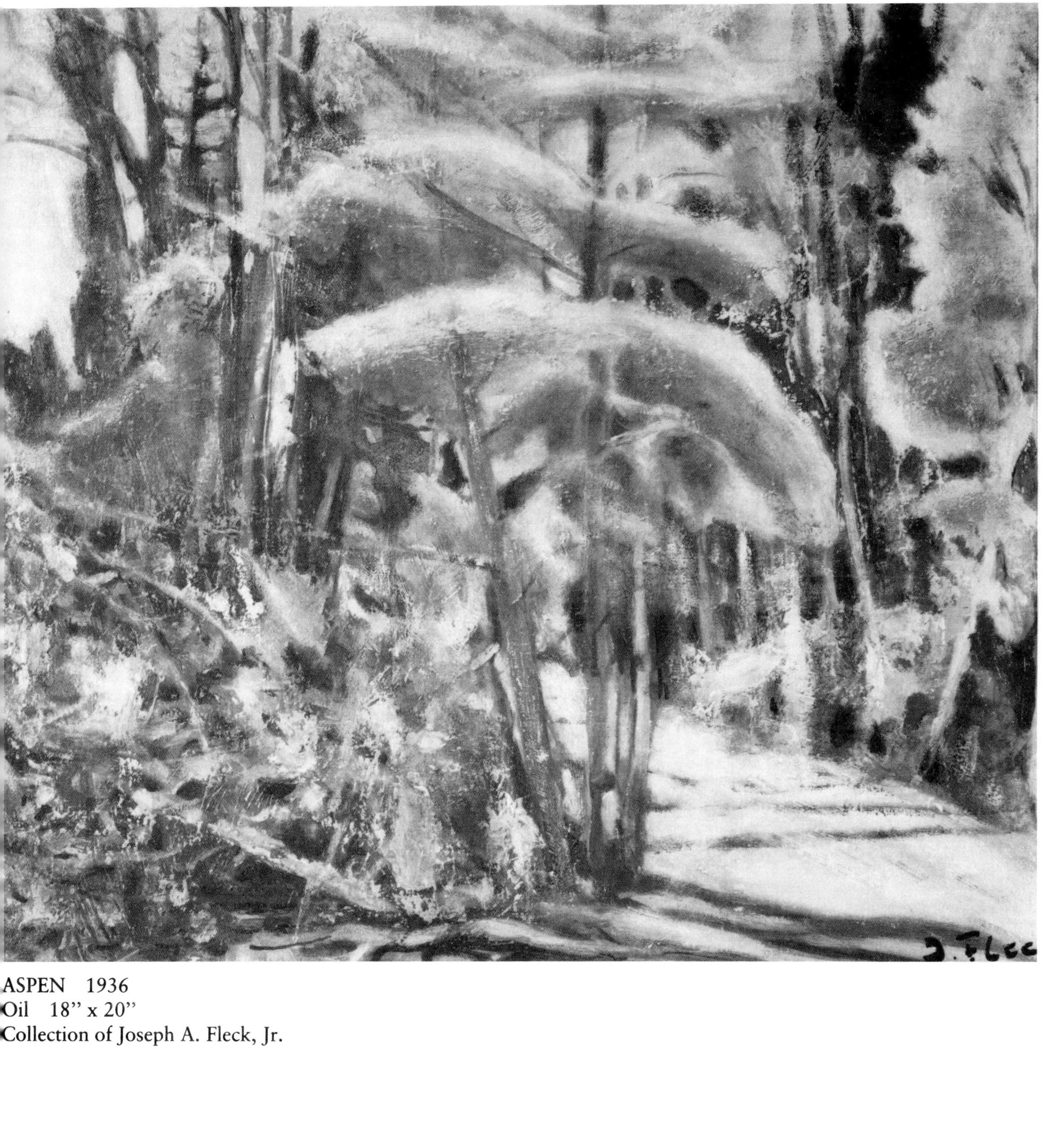

ASPEN 1936
Oil 18" x 20"
Collection of Joseph A. Fleck, Jr.

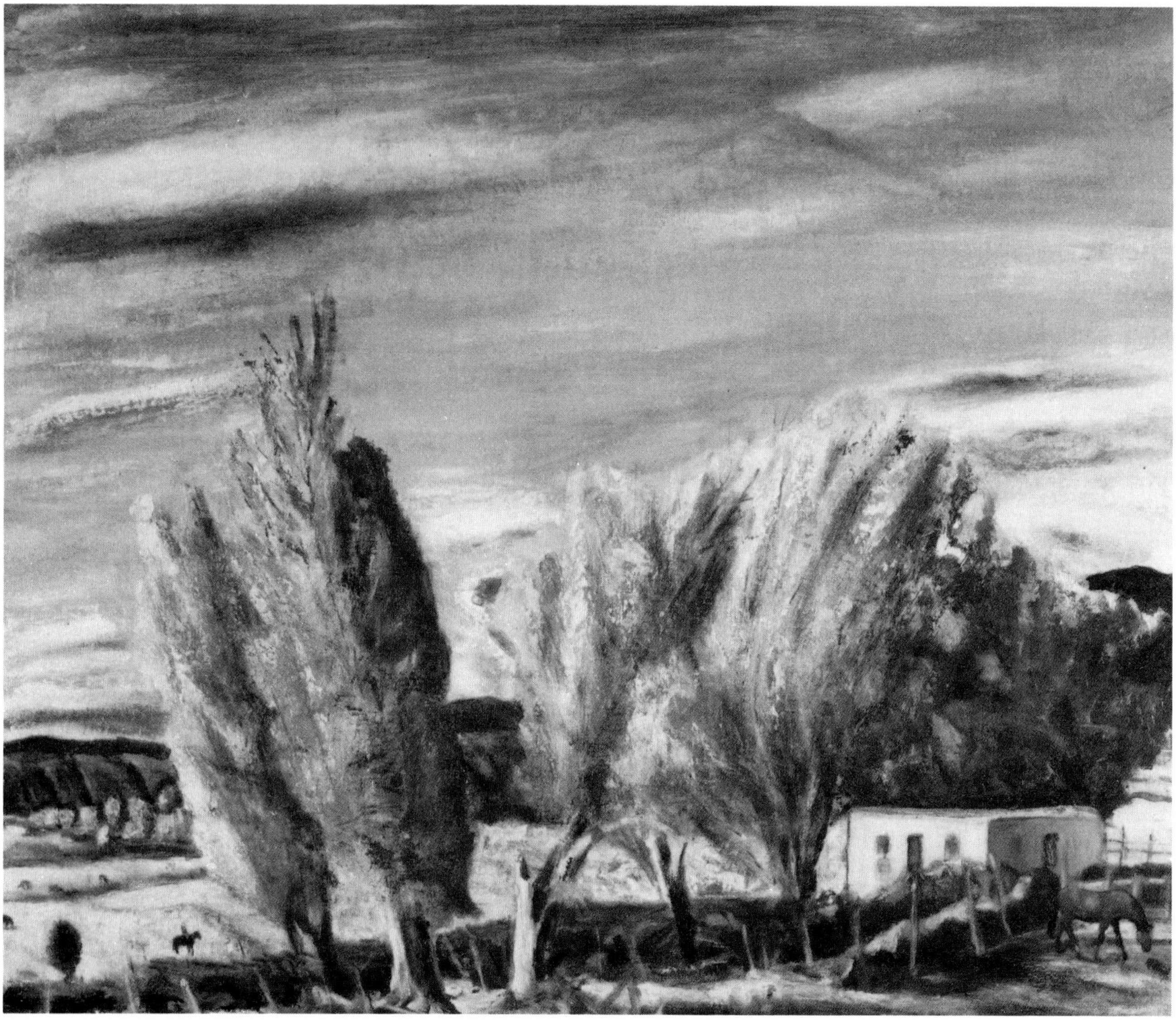

HOUSE IN THE SUNSHINE 1945
Oil 30" x 35"
Collection of Joseph A. Fleck, Jr.

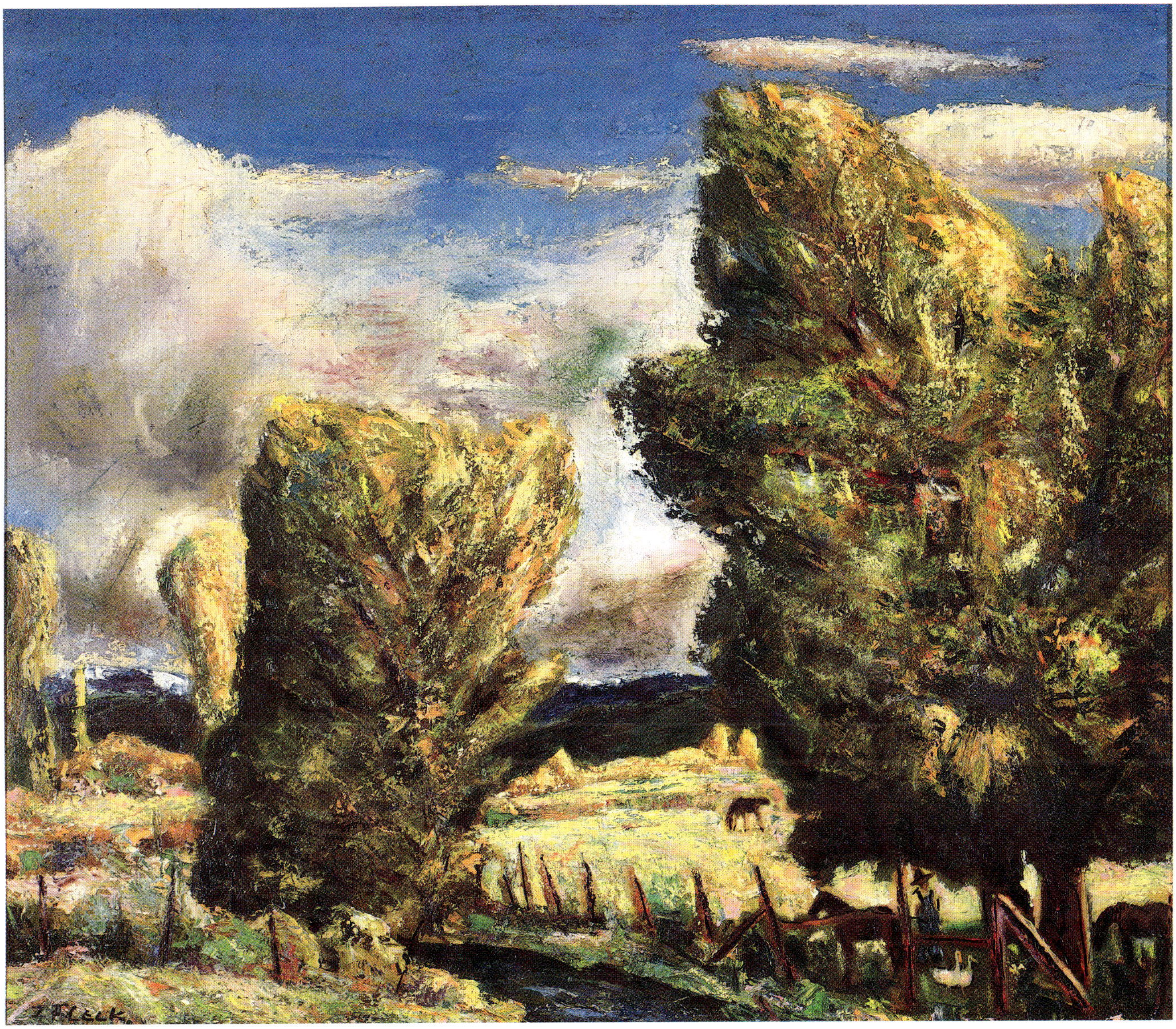

SUMMER PASTORAL 1946
Oil 30" x 36"
Collection of Joseph A. Fleck, Jr.

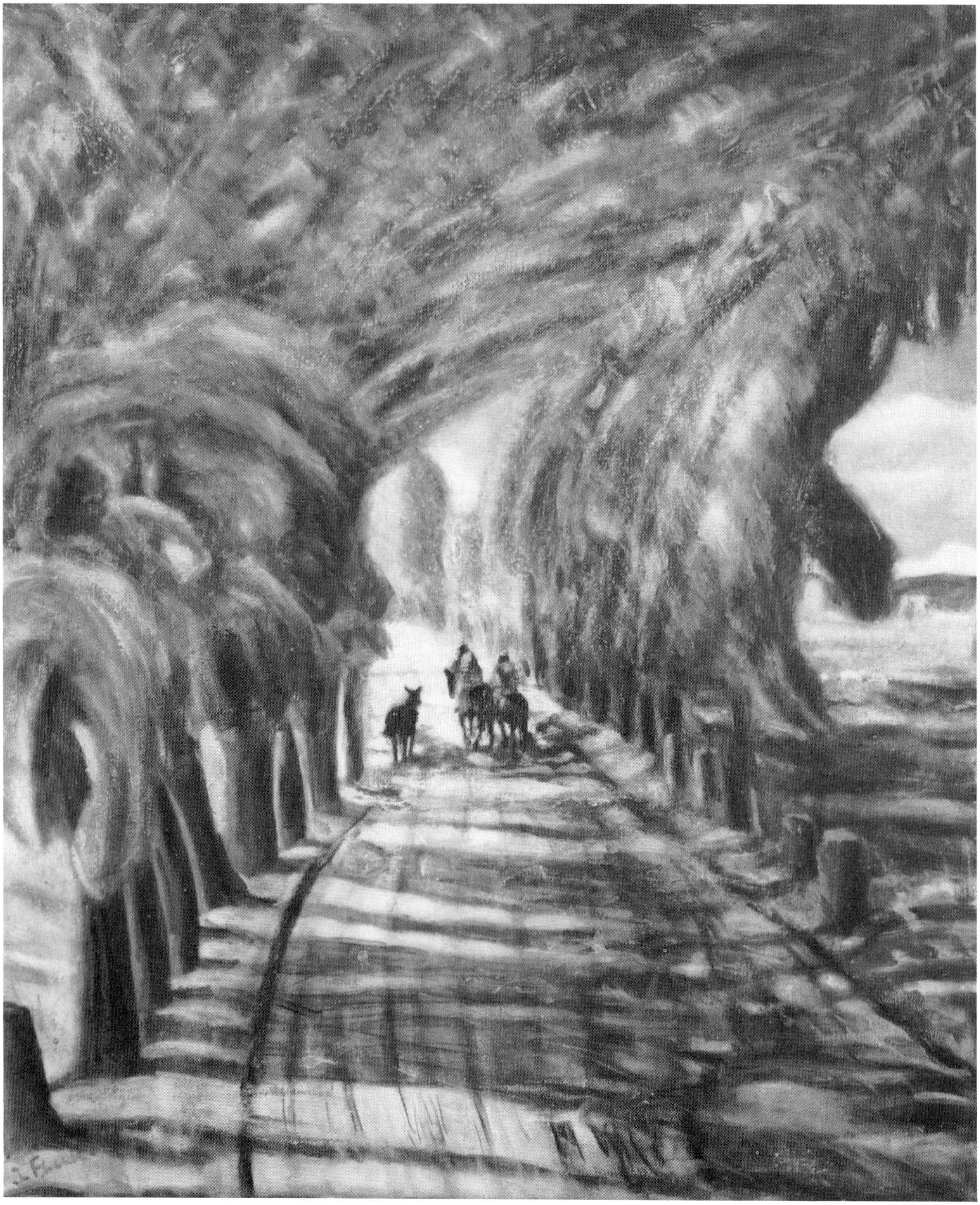

GOING HOME, AUTUMN 1940
Oil 30" x 35"
Collection of Joseph A. Fleck, Jr.

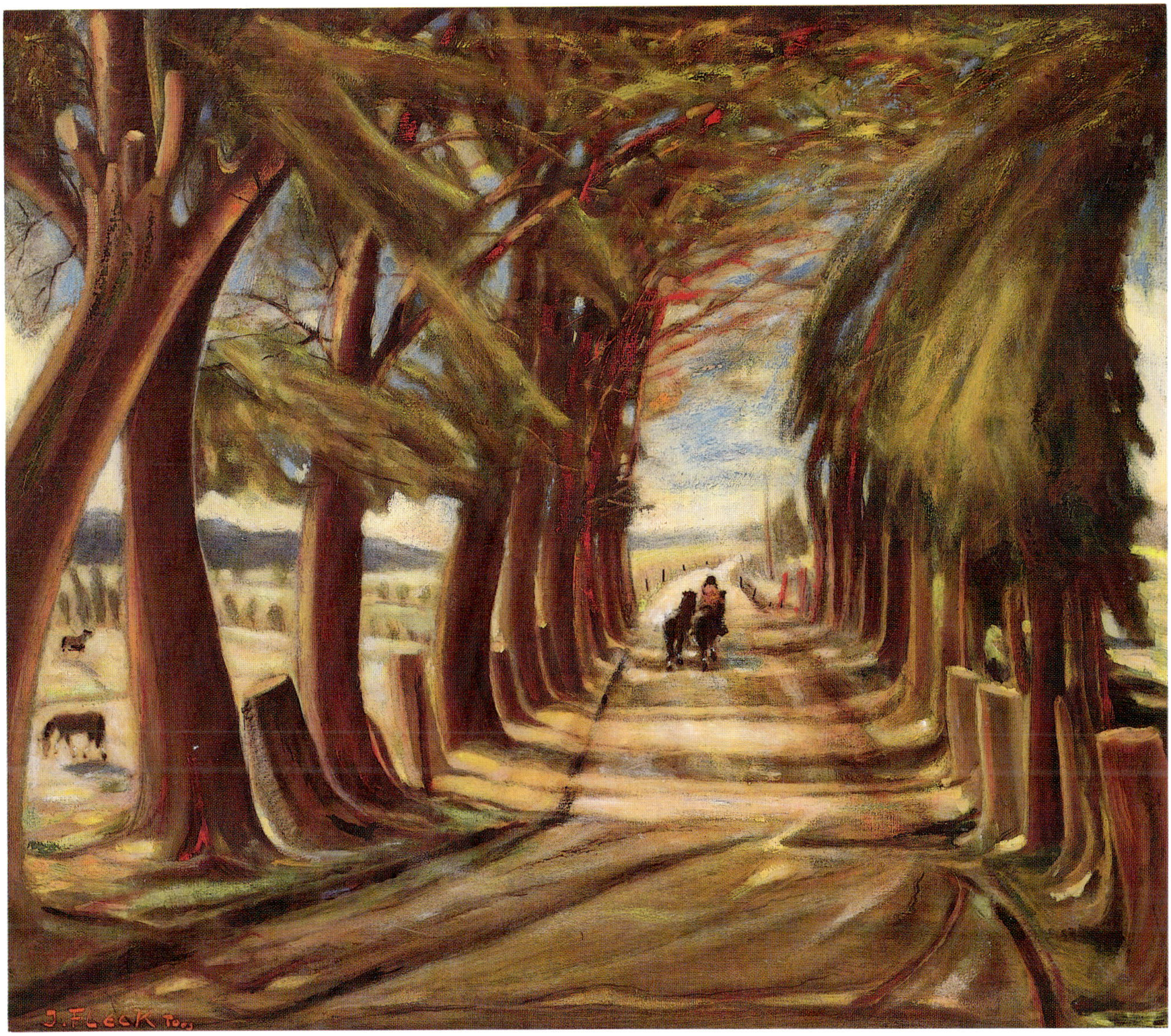

GOING HOME, SUMMER 1940
Oil 30" x 35"
Collection of Joseph A. Fleck, Jr.

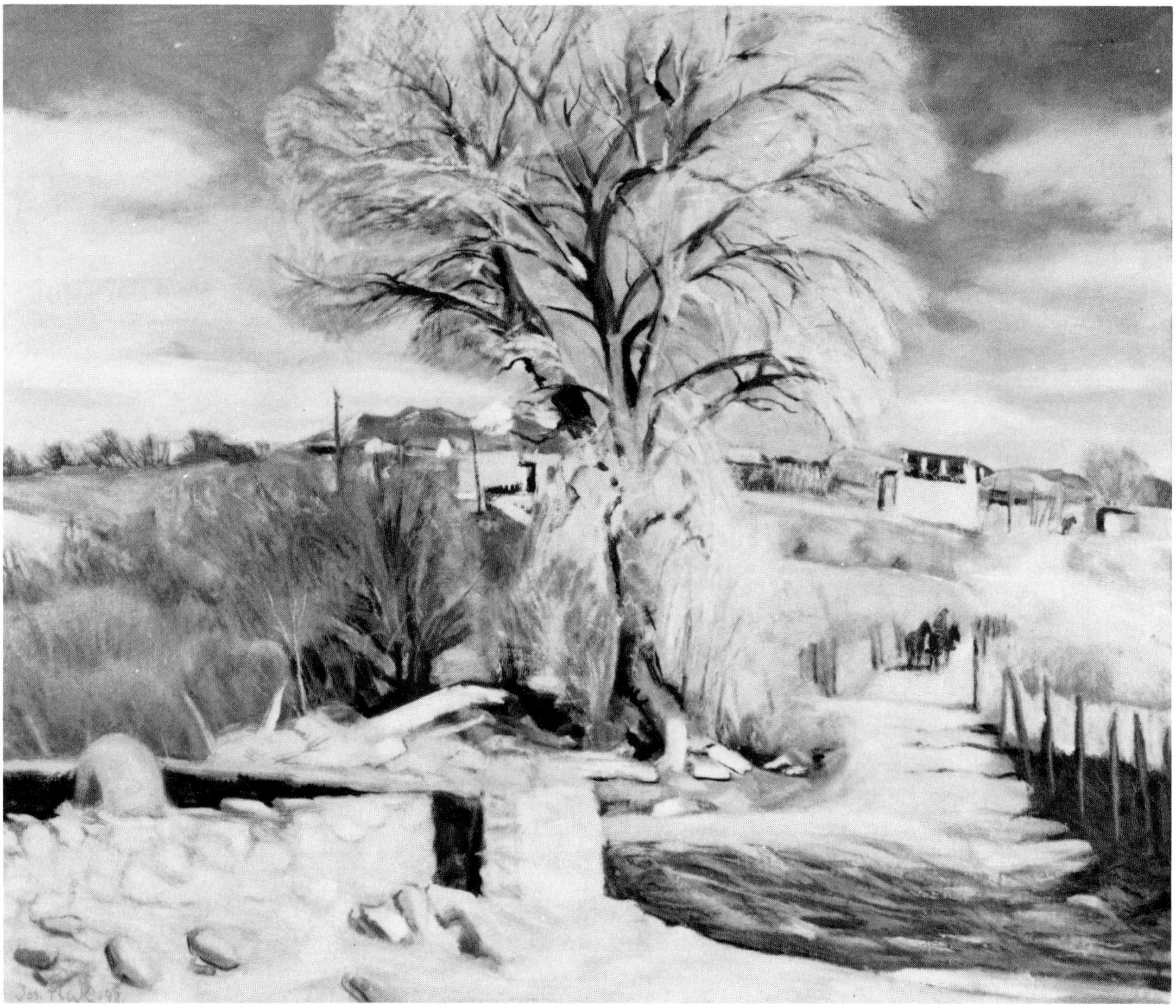

WINTER'S SONG 1948
Oil 25" x 30"
Donated by the Oklahoma Art League to the
Oklahoma Art Center Permanent Collection

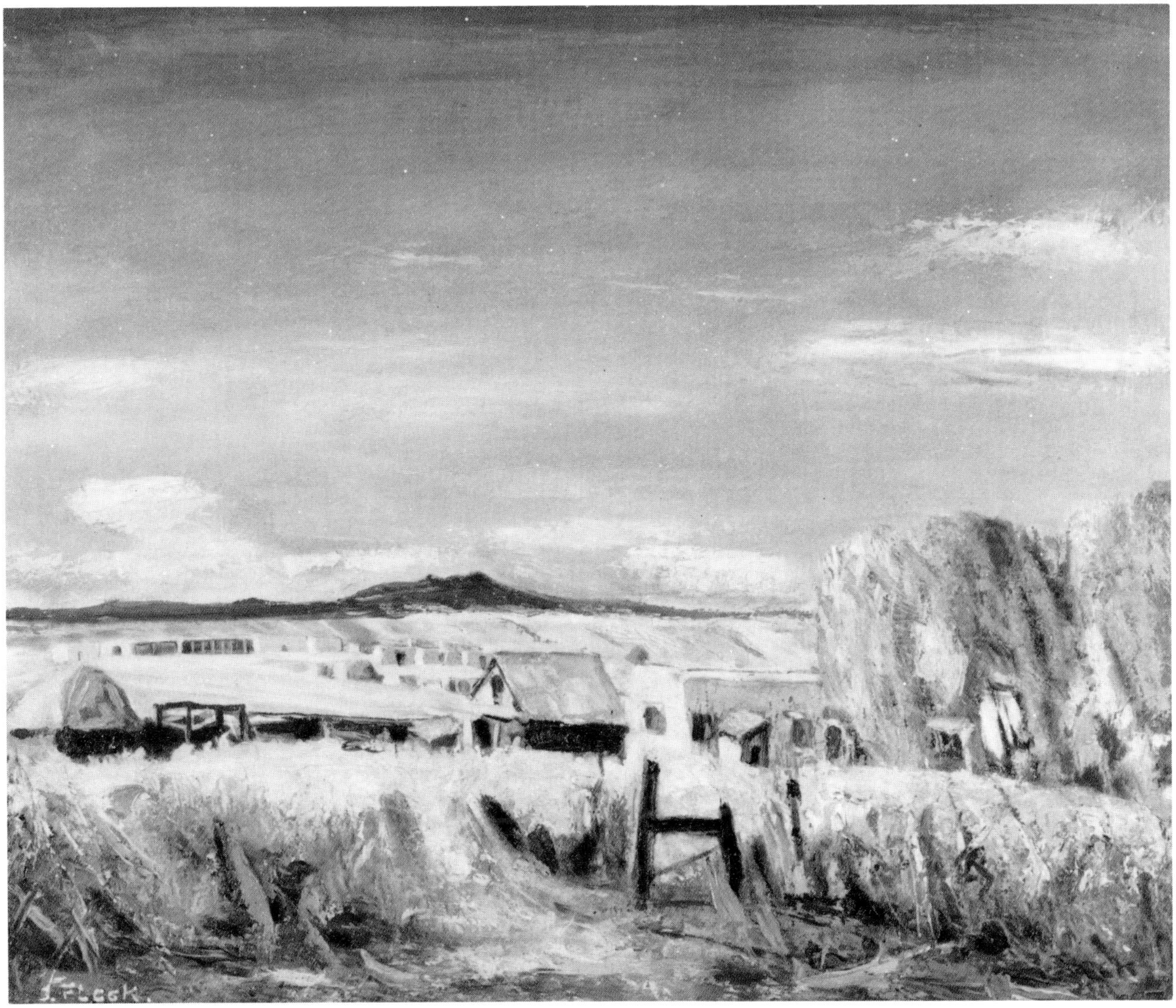

AUTUMN, TALPA LANDSCAPE 1948
Oil 20" x 24"
Collection of Joseph A. Fleck, Jr.

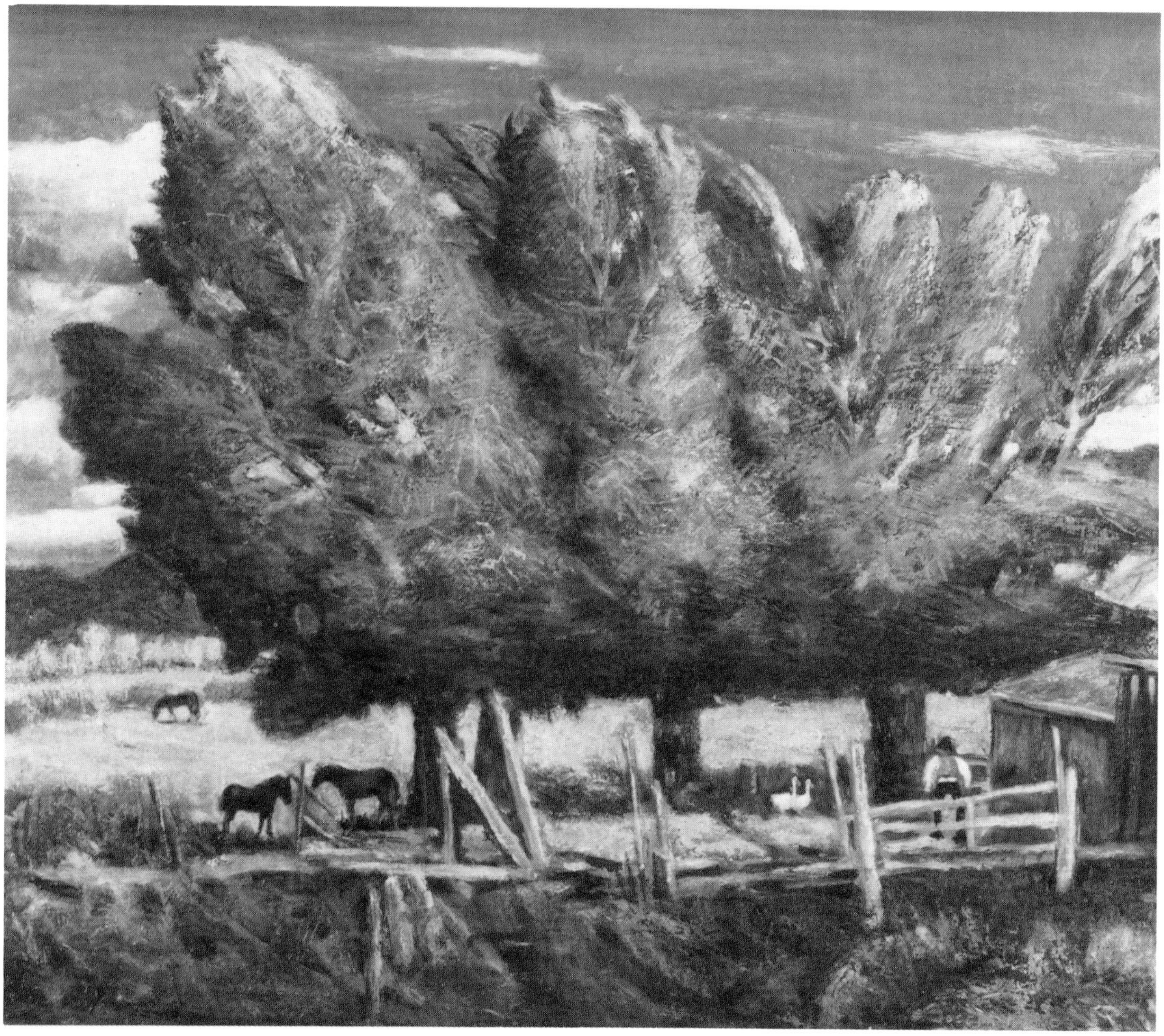

SUMMER DAY 1946
Oil 35" x 36"
Collection of Joseph A. Fleck, Jr.

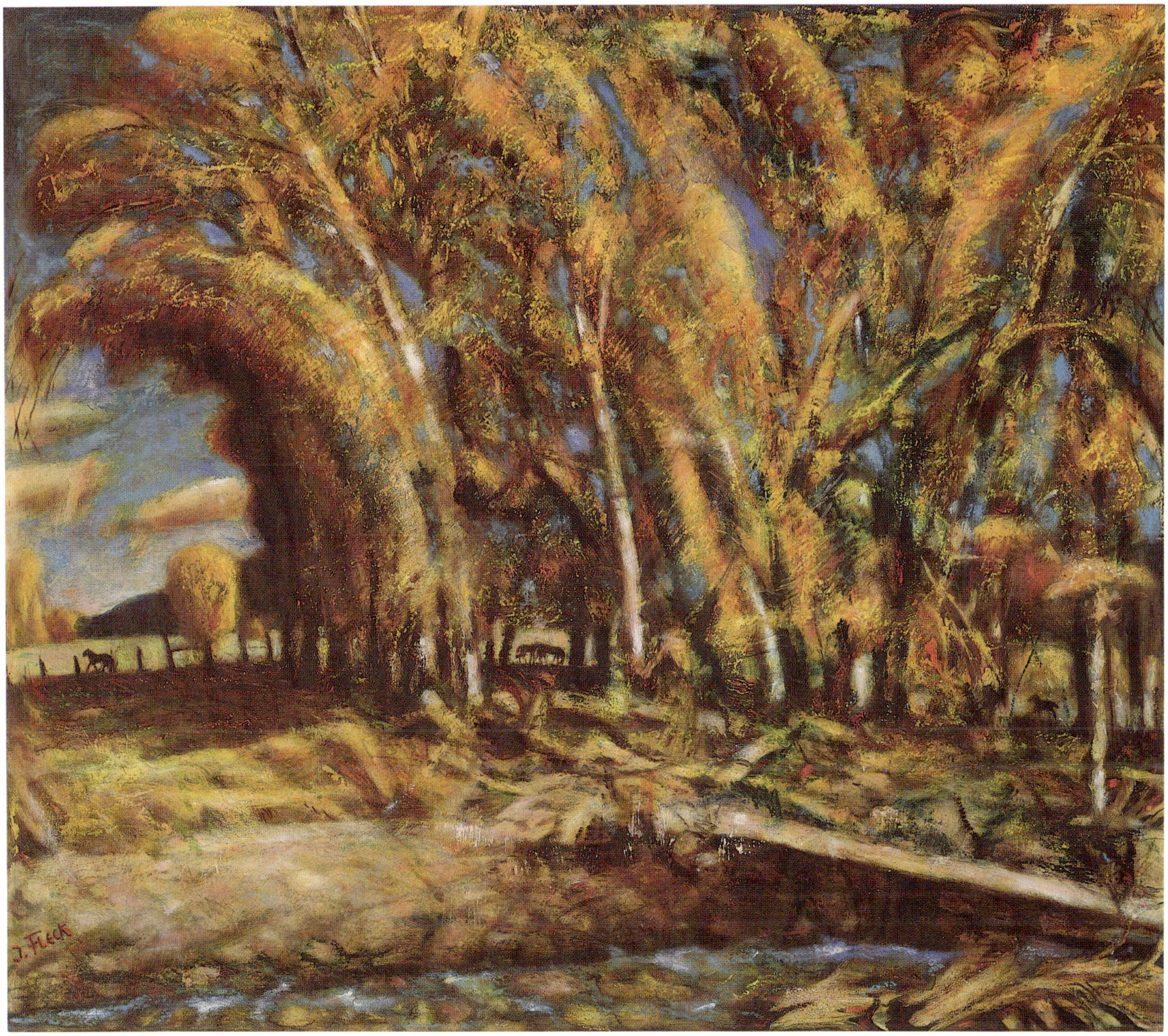

AFTER THE STORM, AUTUMN WIND 1946
Oil 30" x 35"
Collection of Joseph A. Fleck, Jr.

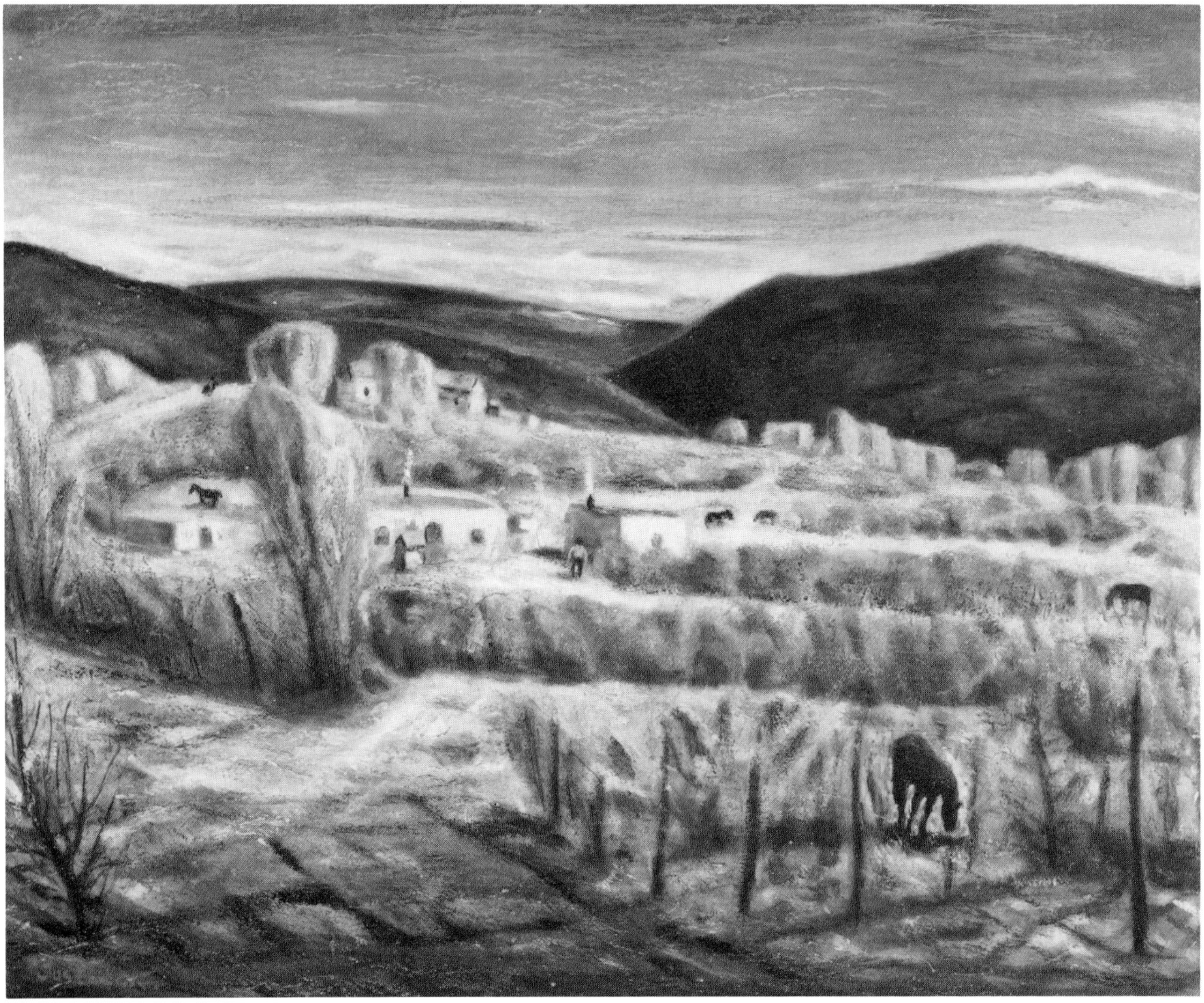

THE TRANQUIL PLACE 1947
Oil 28" x 34"
Collection of Joseph A. Fleck, Jr.

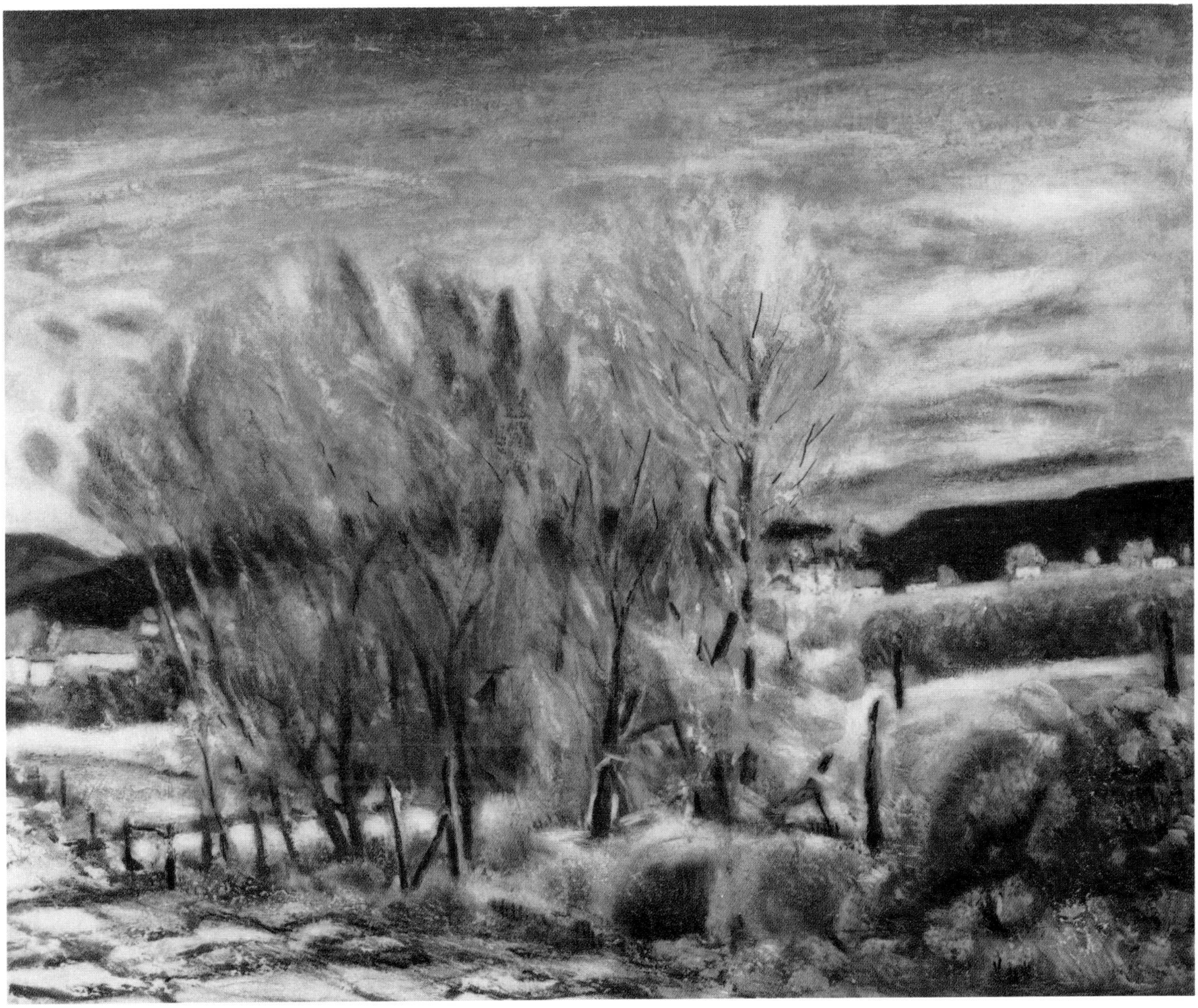

AUTUMN ECSTASY 1950
Oil 28" x 34"
Collection of Joseph A. Fleck, Jr.

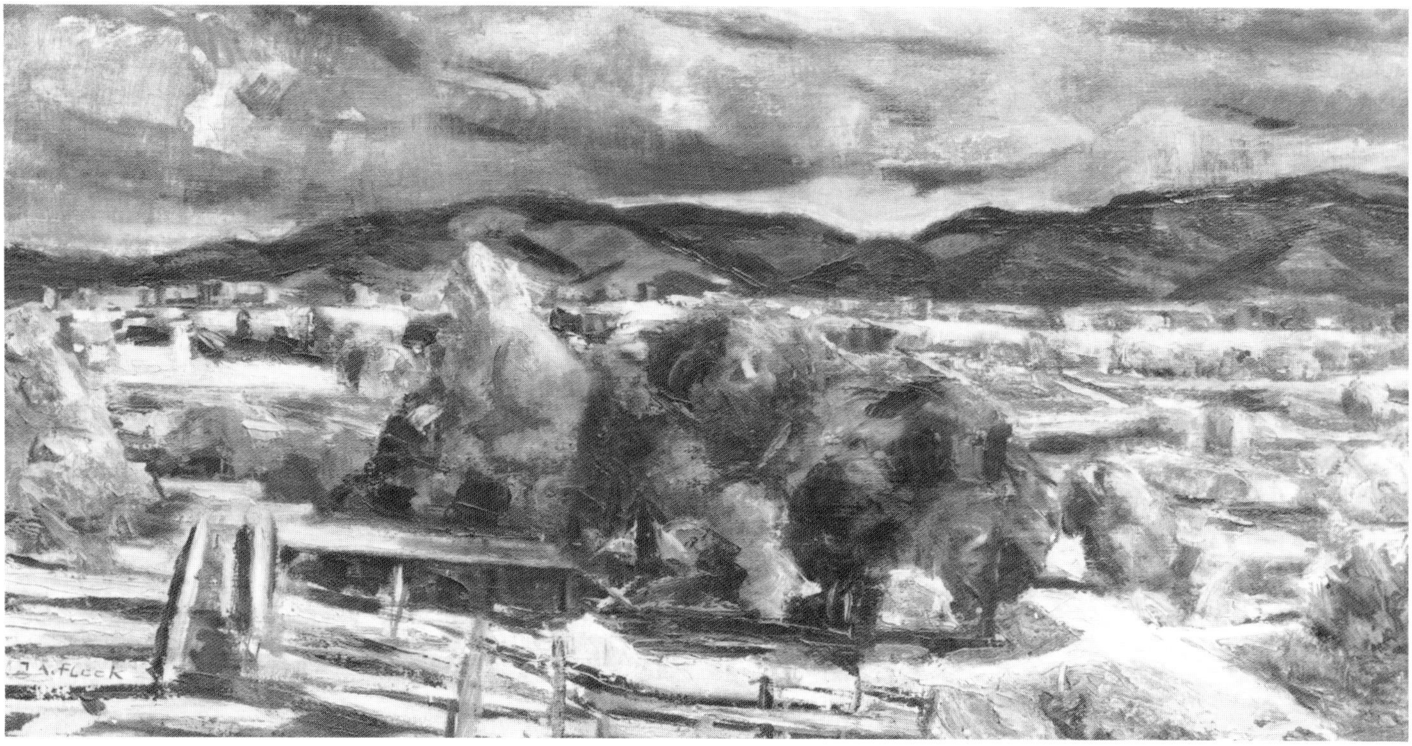

APPROACHING STORM 1960
Oil 18" x 36"
Permanent Collection of the New Mexico
State Fair

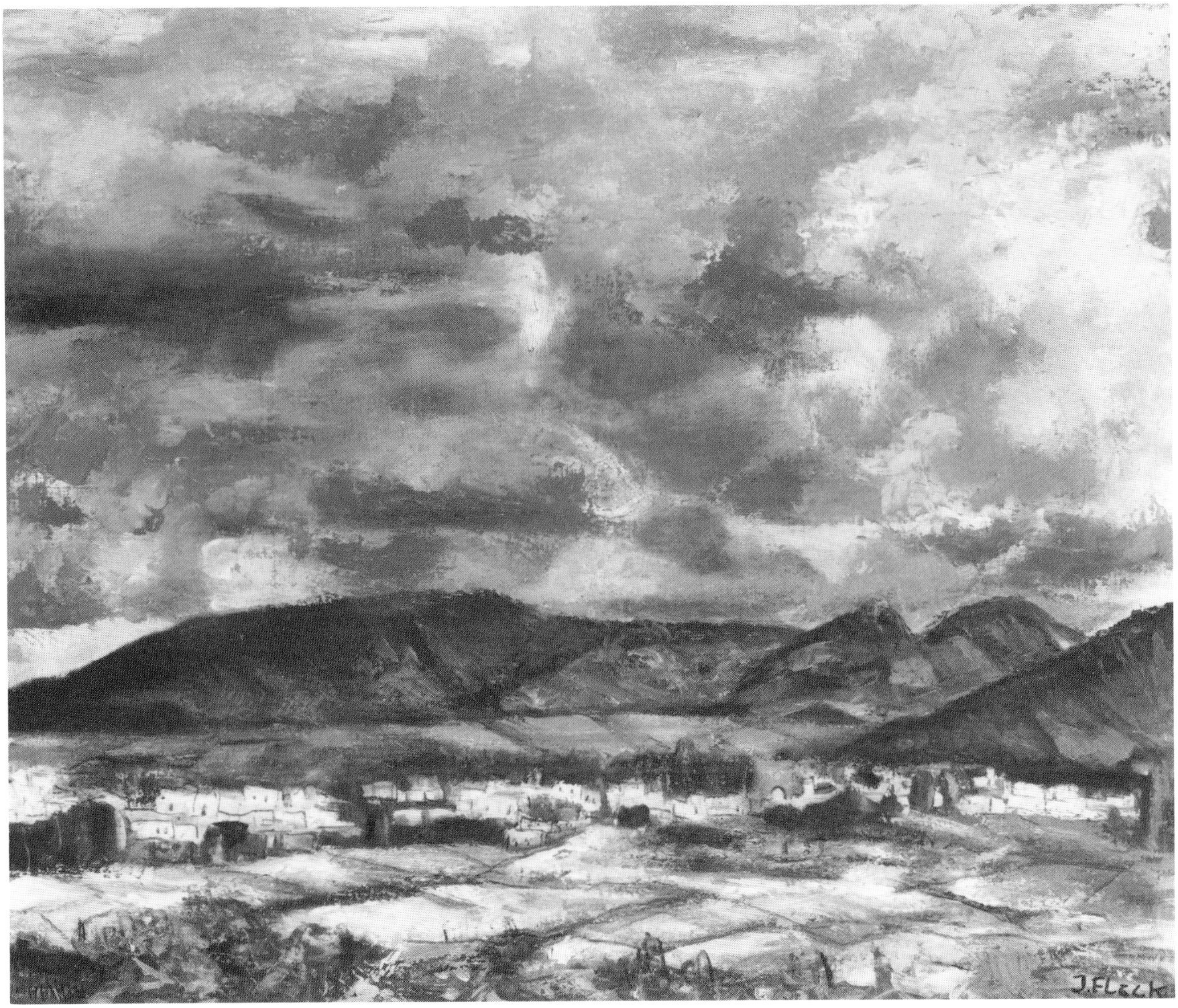

VISTA OF RAIN 1960
Oil 25" x 30"
Collection of Joseph A. Fleck, Jr.

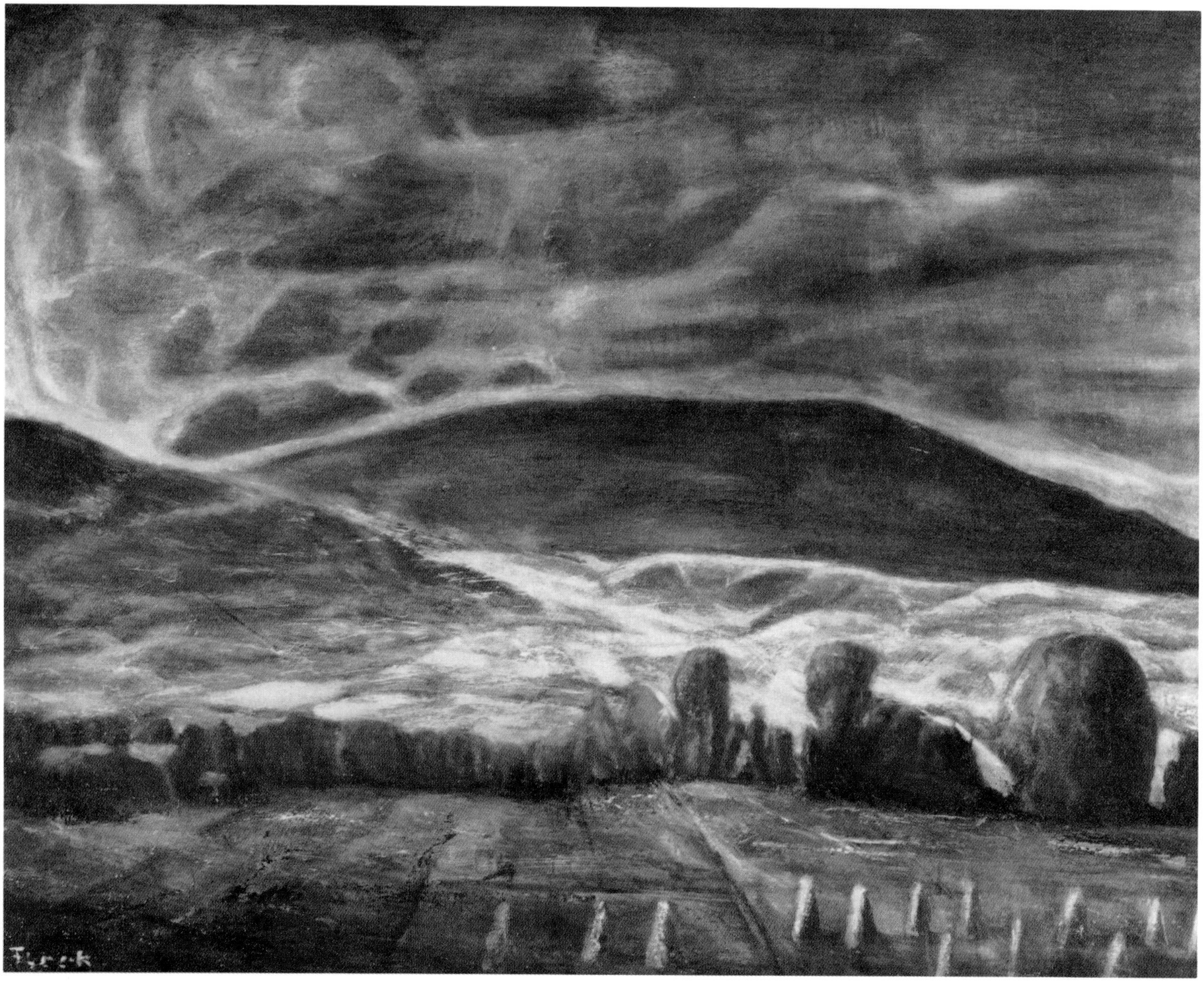

THE HARVEST 1956
Oil 28" x 35"
Collection of Joseph A. Fleck, Jr.

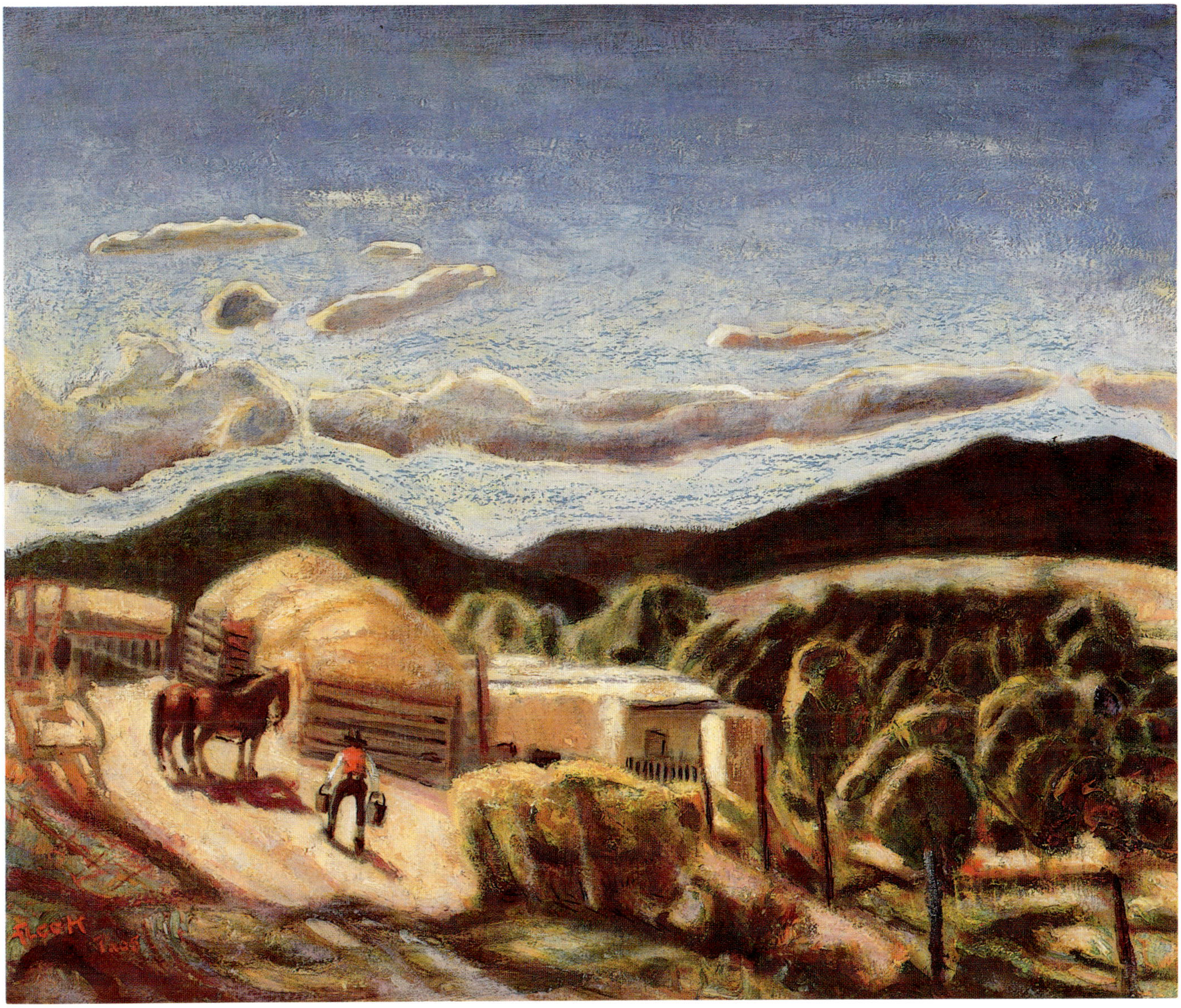

NEW MEXICO LANDSCAPE 1948
Oil 25" x 30"
Collection of Joseph A. Fleck, Jr.

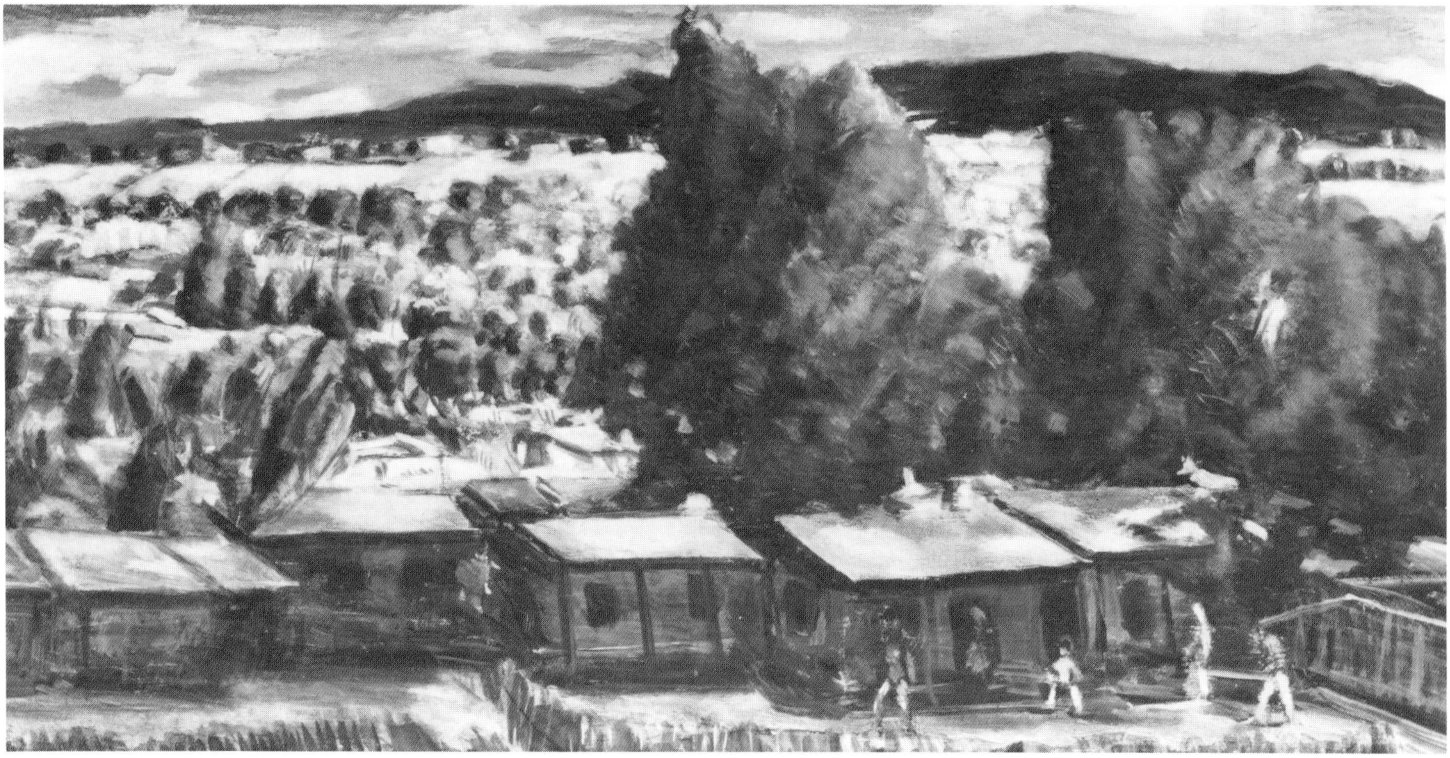

FIGURES IN THE SHADOW 1962
Oil 18" x 36"
Collection of Joseph A. Fleck, Jr.

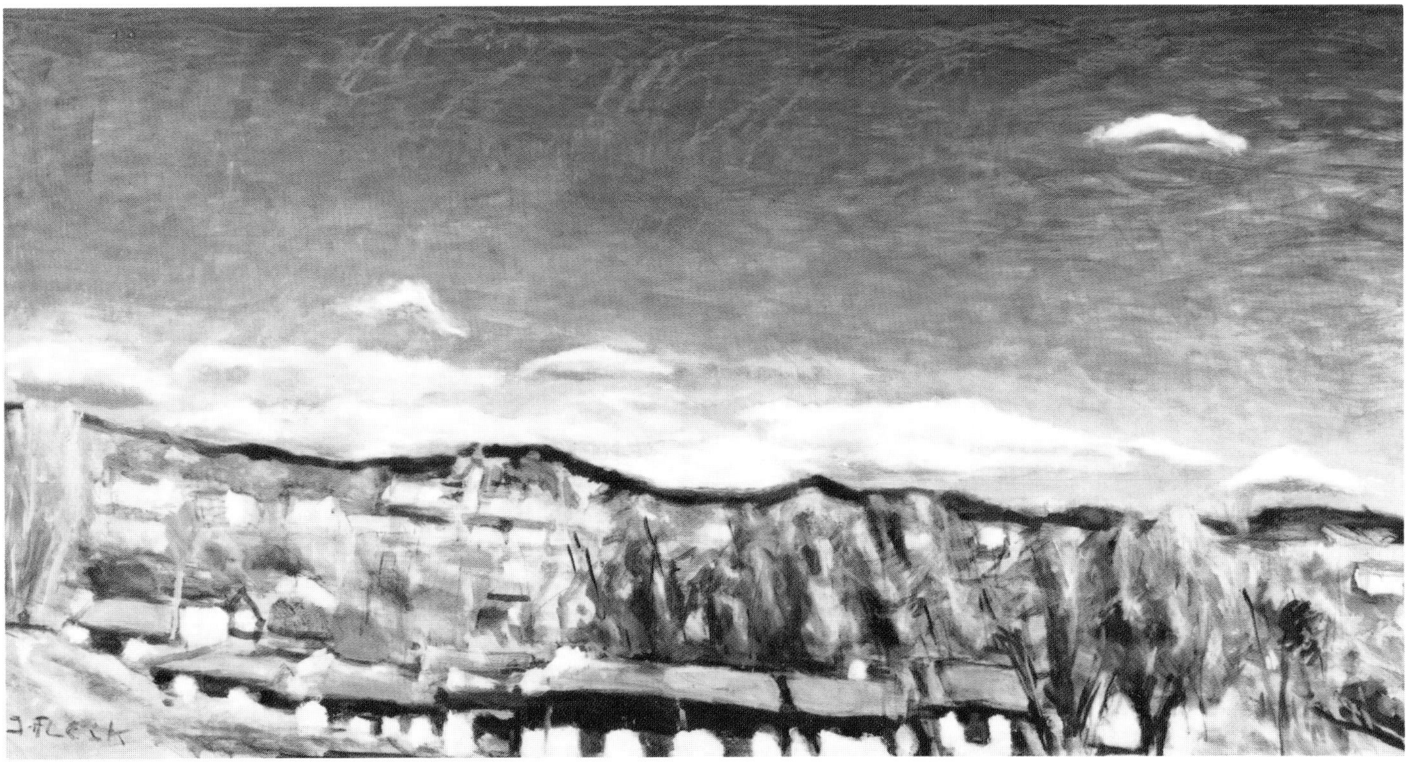

EARLY SPRING IN LLANO 1966
Oil 18" x 36"
Collection of Joseph A. Fleck, Jr.

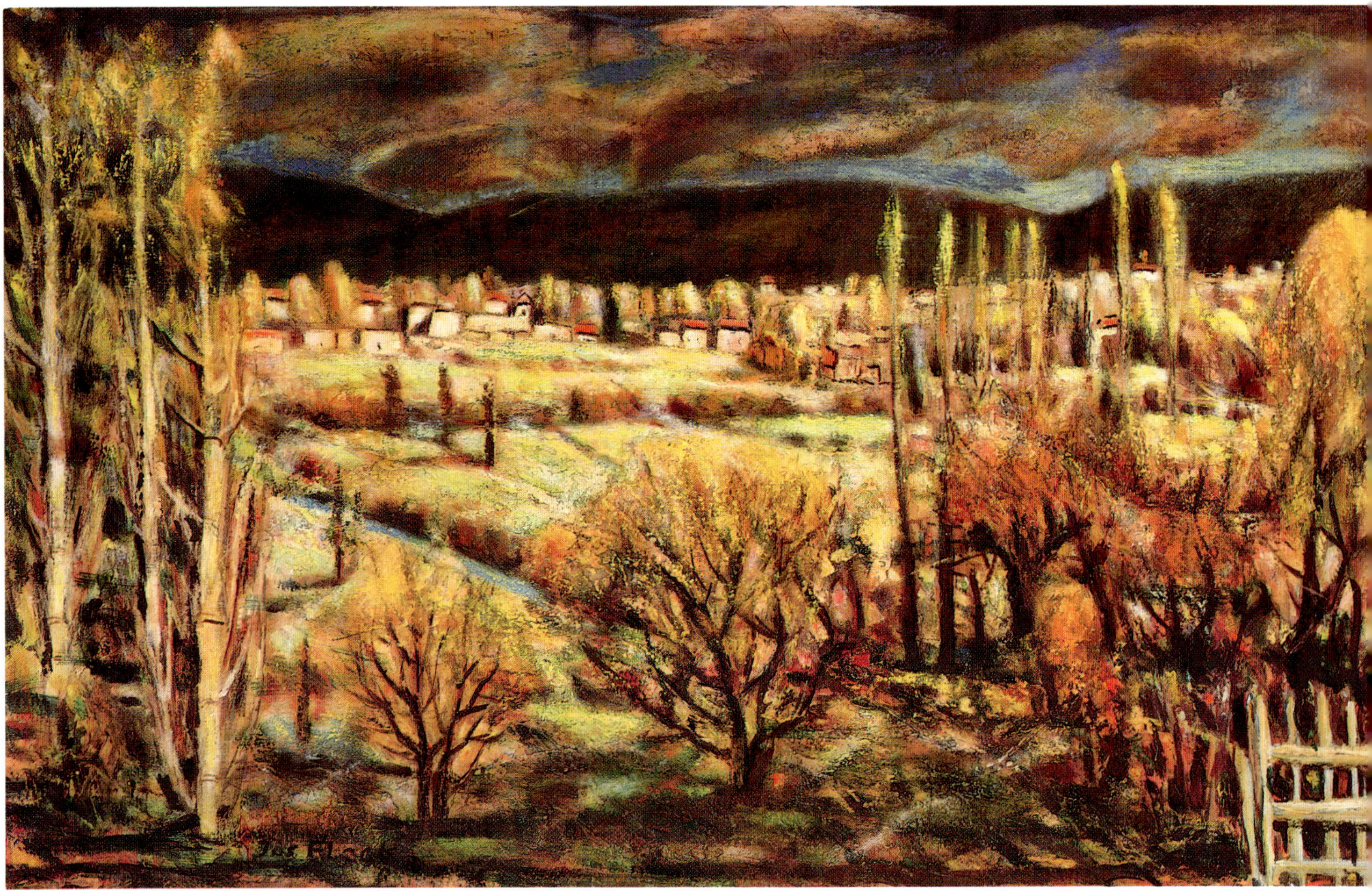

AUTUMN IN THE VALLEY 1955
Oil 23" x 36"
Collection of Joseph A. Fleck, Jr.

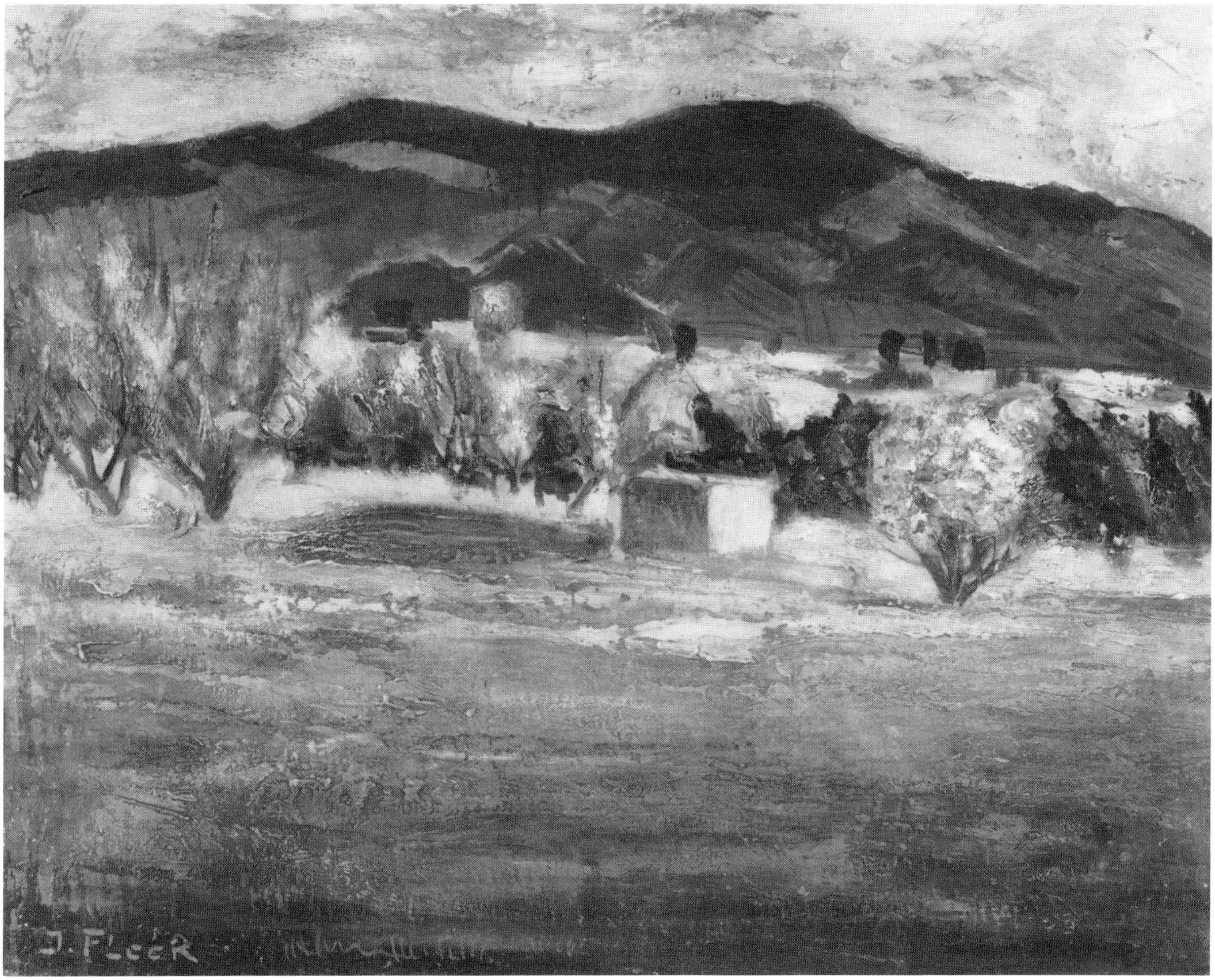

SPRINGTIME 1968
Oil 14" x 18"
Collection of Joseph A. Fleck, Jr.

Checklist

AFTER THE STORM, AUTUMN WIND 1946
Oil 30" x 35"
Collection of Joseph A. Fleck, Jr.
Page 47

AMARILLA 1930
Oil 30" x 25"
The Carl and Elisabeth Waldo Dentzel Collection
Page 28

APPROACHING STORM 1960
Oil 18" x 36"
Permanent Collection of the New Mexico State Fair
Page 50

ASPEN 1936
Oil 18" x 20"
Collection of Joseph A. Fleck, Jr.
Page 39

AUTUMN, TALPA LANDSCAPE 1948
Oil 20" x 24"
Collection of Joseph A. Fleck, Jr.
Page 45

AUTUMN ECSTASY 1950
Oil 28" x 34"
Collection of Joseph A. Fleck, Jr.
Page 49

AUTUMN IN THE VALLEY 1955
Oil 23" x 36"
Collection of Joseph A. Fleck, Jr.
Page 56

THE CELLO PLAYER 1944
Oil 30" x 25"
Collection of Joseph A. Fleck, Jr.
Page 34

EARLY SPRING IN LLANO 1966
Oil 18" x 36"
Collection of Joseph A. Fleck, Jr.
Page 55

FIESTA ARRAY 1929
Oil 50" x 46"
The Carl and Elisabeth Waldo Dentzel Collection
Cover

FIGURES IN THE SHADOW 1962
Oil 18" x 36"
Collection of Joseph A. Fleck, Jr.
Page 54

FLYING CLOUD 1934
Oil 12" x 16"
Collection of Joseph A. Fleck, Jr.
Page 31

GIRL WITH MANTILLA 1933
Oil 24" x 20"
Collection of Lewis L. Dail
Page 38

GOING HOME, AUTUMN 1940
Oil 30" x 35"
Collection of Joseph A. Fleck, Jr.
Page 42

GOING HOME, SUMMER 1940
Oil 30" x 35"
Collection of Joseph A. Fleck, Jr.
Page 43

THE GUITARIST 1938
Oil 35⅛" x 32"
Collection of the Museum of Fine Arts, Museum of New Mexico
Page 32

THE HARVEST 1956
Oil 28" x 35"
Collection of Joseph A. Fleck, Jr.
Page 52

HONDO CANYON, LOOKING WEST 1938
Oil 24" x 32"
Collection of Michael J. Ross
Page 30

HOUSE IN THE SUN 1924
Oil 13⅝" x 13⅝"
Collection of Mr. and Mrs. Robert E. McKee III
Page 24

HOUSE IN THE SUNSHINE 1945
Oil 30" x 35"
Collection of Joseph A. Fleck, Jr.
Page 40

INDIAN BRIDE 1935
Oil 31" x 45"
Collection of Joseph A. Fleck, Jr.
Page 27

INDIAN SUMMER 1929
Oil 32½" x 35¼"
Collection of Mr. and Mrs. Joseph Szymanski
Page 25

MEXICAN BOTTLER 1926
Oil 33" x 29"
Collection of Joseph A. Fleck, Jr.
Page 20

NEW MEXICO LANDSCAPE 1948
Oil 25" x 30"
Collection of Joseph A. Fleck, Jr.
Page 53

OLD SPANISH HOME 1925
Oil 24" x 27"
Collection of the El Paso Museum of Art
Page 22

PEACEFUL HUNT 1936
Oil 25" x 30"
The Harmsen Collection
Page 6

PORTRAIT OF THE ARTIST'S SON 1932
Oil 12" x 18"
Collection of Joseph A. Fleck, Jr.
Page 36

PORTRAIT OF THE ARTIST'S WIFE 1951
Oil 20" x 24"
Collection of Joseph A. Fleck, Jr.
Page 37

PORTRAIT OF NOULA 1938
Oil 32" x 27"
Collection of The Harwood Foundation Museum of Taos Art
Page 35

POTTERY GIRL 1929
Oil 31" x 27½"
Collection of Mr. and Mrs. Robert E. McKee III
Page 29
This painting will only be exhibited in Santa Fe and Roswell.

ROSITA 1931
Oil 18" x 17¼"
The Nelson-Atkins Museum of Art, gift from the Howard P. Treadway and Tertia F. Treadway Collection
Page 21

SPANISH COWBOY 1925
Oil 25" x 30"
Collection of Western Art and Artifacts of Business Men's Assurance Company of America
Page 23

SPRINGTIME 1968
Oil 14" x 18"
Collection of Joseph A. Fleck, Jr.
Page 57

SUMMER DAY 1946
Oil 35" x 36"
Collection of Joseph A. Fleck, Jr.
Page 46

SUMMER PASTORAL 1946
Oil 30" x 36"
Collection of Joseph A. Fleck, Jr.
Page 41

SUNNY CORNER 1925
Oil 30" x 25"
Collection of Michael J. Ross
Page 14

THE TRANQUIL PLACE 1947
Oil 28" x 34"
Collection of Joseph A. Fleck, Jr.
Page 48

TWO SPANISH MUSICIANS 1938
Oil 30¼" x 43¾"
Collection of the University Art Museum, University of New Mexico
Page 33

VISTA OF RAIN 1960
Oil 25" x 30"
Collection of Joseph A. Fleck, Jr.
Page 51

WINTER'S SONG 1948
Oil 25" x 30"
Donated by the Oklahoma Art League to the Oklahoma Art Center Permanent Collection
Page 44

YOUNG MAN WITH SOMBRERO 1931
Oil 20" x 24"
Collection of Joseph A. Fleck, Jr.
Page 26

Chronology

1892 Born to Joseph Amadeus and Barbara Reisner Fleck in Sziklos, Austria-Hungary, later to become Siegless in the province of Burgenland, Austria.

1900 Moved to Vienna with family.

1906 Apprenticed to an ornamental engraver.

1910 Executed, as his masterwork to complete apprenticeship, a bas-relief of Emperor Franz Joseph.

1912 Entered Royal Academy of Fine Arts after completing two-year course at Institute for Graphic Design.

1914 Interrupted academy studies at outbreak of World War I to serve in Austrio-Hungarian army; became unofficial regimental artist.

1915 Returned to Vienna as officer aspirant; spent remainder of war in Vienna, painting prominent government and military figures.

1918 Awarded medal for valor after preventing bloodshed during barracks uprising, which took place in the brief revolution that toppled the government of Emperor Franz Joseph.

1920 Completed academy studies; decorated world-famous Femina nightclub in Vienna.

1922 Arrived in Kansas City; found job in Tiffany stained-glass factory and became chief designer within a year.

1923 Won Bronze Medal for graphic arts in Kansas City Art Institute exhibition.

1924 Arrived in Taos during summer, after seeing exhibition of paintings by Taos Society of Artists in Kansas City; later returned to Kansas City and exhibited his Taos paintings.

1925 Married Mable Davidson Mantz and returned to Taos permanently.

1926 Embarked on extended European painting tour with wife.

1927 Won Chicago Art Institute's Rosenwald Prize for *Pueblo Flower*.

1928 Won First Prize at Arizona State Fair for *Anita and the Bear;* Joseph, Jr., born.

1929 Won Silver Medal at Midwestern Artists' Exhibition of Kansas City Art Institute for *Child with Doll.*

1930 Embarked on second European painting tour.

1931 Had one-man shows at Galerie Bernheim-Jeune in Paris and three-man show with Joseph Allworthy and Gerald Cassidy at Chicago Galleries Association.

1932 Painted WPA murals and made numerous trips to Texas in search of portrait commissions.

1936 Transported, with Hennings, Walter Ufer—stricken with appendicitis—through Rio Grande Gorge to Santa Fe hospital.

1939 Exhibited *The Guitarist* at New York World's Fair.

1940 Exhibited *Toledo Nocturne* in Forty-Eight States and Canada Traveling Exhibition and *Toledo Bridge* at San Francisco World's Fair.

1942 Showed in two-man exhibit with Sheldon Parsons at Museum of New Mexico; joined faculty of University of Kansas City (now University of Missouri at Kansas City) as Artist in Residence, then Dean of Fine Arts; met Thomas Hart Benton and established close friendship.

1944 Given one-man show at William Rockhill Nelson Museum, Kansas City.

1946 Left University of Kansas City and returned to Taos permanently; Taos Artists Association formed.

1947 Elected president of Taos Artists Association; presided for two years.

1949 Given one-man exhibition at Oklahoma Art Center.

1958 Given juried inaugural exhibition at Oklahoma Art Center.

1962 Given retrospective exhibition at University Art Museum, University of New Mexico.

1965 Awarded First Prize, Grand Award, and Purchase Prize for *Approaching Storm* at New Mexico State Fair.

1967 Honored by addition of *Springtime in the Mountains* to permanent collection of Österreichische Galerie in Vienna's Oberes Belvedere.

1977 Died in Pleasanton, California.

1980 Represented in an exhibition at the Oberes Belvedere's Österreichische Galerie, titled "Die Uns Verliessen" and dedicated to artists lost to Austria through emigration.

Awards, Exhibitions, Collections

Awards

Kansas City Art Institute, Bronze Medal, 1923
Chicago Art Institute, Morris S. Rosenwald Prize, 1927
Arizona State Fair, First Prize, 1928
Kansas City Art Institute, Silver Medal, 1929
Leon Gaspard Memorial Prize, Taos, 1964
New Mexico State Fair, First Prize, Purchase Prize, Grand Award, 1965

Important Juried Exhibitions

Chicago Art Institute, 1925
Los Angeles Art Museum Pan-American Exhibition, 1925
Kansas City Art Institute, 1926
New York Society of Independent Artists, 1926
Kansas City Art Institute, 1926
Cincinnati Art Museum, 1926
Milwaukee Art Museum, 1926
Chicago Art Institute, 1926
Pennsylvania Academy of Fine Arts, Philadelphia, 1926
National Academy of Design, New York, 1927
Carnegie International Exhibition, Pittsburgh, 1928
Corcoran Gallery of Art, Washington, D.C., 1928
Kansas City Art Institute, 1929
Buffalo Fine Arts Academy, 1929
Chicago Art Institute, 1931
Pennsylvania Academy of Fine Arts, 1931
John H. Vanderpoel Art Gallery, Chicago, 1931
John H. Vanderpoel Art Gallery, Chicago, 1932
Pennsylvania Academy of Fine Arts, 1933
Pennsylvania Academy of Fine Arts, 1935
Fort Worth Frontier Centennial Exposition, 1936
National Academy of Design, New York, 1936
Chicago Art Institute, 1937
Pennsylvania Academy of Fine Arts, 1938
Toledo Museum of Art, Ohio, 1938
New York World's Fair, 1939
San Francisco World's Fair, 1940
Forty-Eight States and Canada Traveling Exhibition, Association of American Artists, 1940
Oklahoma Art Center Inaugural Exhibition, Oklahoma City, 1958

Important One-Man and Group Shows

Kansas City Art Institute, 1929
Museum of Fine Arts, Houston, 1930
Breckenridge Museum, San Antonio, 1930
Galerie Bernheim-Jeune, Paris, 1931
Chicago Galleries Association (three-man show with Joseph Allworthy and Gerald Cassidy), 1931
Museum of Fine Arts, Museum of New Mexico, Santa Fe (two-man show with Sheldon Parsons), 1942
William Rockhill Nelson Museum, Kansas City, Missouri, 1944
Oklahoma Art Center, 1949
Museum of Fine Arts, Museum of New Mexico, Santa Fe, 1954
University Art Museum, University of New Mexico, Albuquerque (retrospective exhibition), 1962
Stables Art Gallery, Taos, 1971
Österreichische Galerie, Oberes Belvedere, Vienna ("Die Uns Verliessen" group exhibition), 1980

Museum Collections

Witte Museum, Art League Collection, San Antonio, *The Melting Pot*
Fort Worth Art Center, *Jim Mirabal*
Museum of New Mexico, Santa Fe, *The Guitarist*
University Art Museum, University of New Mexico, Albuquerque, *Two Spanish Musicians*
The Harwood Foundation Museum of Taos Art, *Portrait of Noula*
The Nelson-Atkins Museum, Kansas City, Missouri, *Rosita*
Kansas City Public Library, Missouri, *Indian Motherhood*
Confederate Museum, Richmond, *Portrait of General Paxton*
Oklahoma Art Center, Oklahoma City, *Winter's Song*
New Mexico State Fair, Permanent Collection, *Approaching Storm*
Österreichische Galerie, Oberes Belvedere, Vienna, *Springtime in the Mountains*
Roswell Museum and Art Center, *Taos Landscape*
Philbrook Art Center, Tulsa, *Taos Pueblo Child*
El Paso Museum of Art, *Old Spanish Home*
Dallas Museum of Fine Arts, *Pueblo*

Murals

Post Office, Raton, New Mexico
Post Office, Hugo, Oklahoma
University of Missouri at Kansas City
Church Altar Painting, Our Lady of Refuge Church, Refugio, Texas

Exhibition Itinerary

June 1–September 22, 1985	Museum of Fine Arts, Museum of New Mexico Santa Fe, New Mexico
October 21–December 9, 1985	Roswell Museum and Art Center Roswell, New Mexico
January 5–February 23, 1986	Oklahoma Art Center Oklahoma City, Oklahoma
April 3–May 30, 1986	Museum of Art of the American West Houston, Texas
July 6–August 24, 1986	Museum of the Southwest Midland, Texas
September 21–November 16, 1986	Panhandle-Plains Historical Museum Canyon, Texas
January 6–February 22, 1987	McAllen International Museum McAllen, Texas

Exhibition Lenders

The Collection of Western Art and Artifacts of Business Men's Assurance Company of America	Kansas City, Missouri
Lewis L. Dail	Kansas City, Missouri
The Carl and Elisabeth Waldo Dentzel Collection	Northridge, California
El Paso Museum of Art	El Paso, Texas
Joseph A. Fleck, Jr.	Livermore, California
The Harmsen Collection	Denver, Colorado
The Harwood Foundation Museum of Taos Art	Taos, New Mexico
Mr. and Mrs. Robert E. McKee III	Dallas, Texas
The Nelson-Atkins Museum of Art	Kansas City, Missouri
New Mexico State Fair	Albuquerque, New Mexico
Oklahoma Art Center	Oklahoma City, Oklahoma
Michael J. Ross	St. Louis, Missouri
Mr. and Mrs. Joseph Szymanski	Pasadena, California
University Art Museum, University of New Mexico	Albuquerque, New Mexico

Catalog Design: Daniel Martinez